DUQUESNE STUDIES

Philosophical Series

11

ENCOUNTER

DUQUESNE STUDIES

Philosophical Series

11

ENCOUNTER

by

REMY C. KWANT, O.S.A., Ph.D.

Translated by

ROBERT C. ADOLFS, O.S.A.

Duquesne University Press, Pittsburgh, Pa.
Editions E. Nauwelaerts, Louvain
1960

Library of Congress Catalog Card Number: 60–11778

Title of the original Dutch edition: *Wijsbegeerte van de Ontmoeting,*
© 1959 by Het Spectrum.

IV

DUQUESNE STUDIES

PHILOSOPHICAL SERIES

Andrew G. van Melsen, D.Sc., D.Ed., and Henry J. Koren, C.S.Sp., S.T.D., Editors.

Volume One—Andrew G. van Melsen, FROM ATOMOS TO ATOM. Pp. XII and 240. Price: paper $3.50, cloth $4.25. Published also in Dutch, German, Spanish, and Italian.

Volume Two—Andrew G. van Melsen, THE PHILOSOPHY OF NATURE. Pp. XII and 263. Second edition, third impression. Price: paper $3.75, cloth $4.50. Published also in Dutch and Italian. Polish edition in preparation.

Volume Three—P. Henry van Laer, PHILOSOPHICO-SCIENTIFIC PROBLEMS. Out of print.

Volume Four—Cajetan, THE ANALOGY OF NAMES and THE CONCEPT OF BEING. Pp. X and 95. Second edition. Price: cloth $2.25.

Volume Five—Louis de Raeymaeker and Others, TRUTH AND FREEDOM. Pp. VII and 132. Second impression. Price: cloth $3.00. Published also in French.

Volume Six—P. Henry van Laer, THE PHILOSOPHY OF SCIENCE. Part One: SCIENCE IN GENERAL. Pp. XVII and 164. Price: paper $3.00, cloth $3.75.

Volume Seven—Stephan Strasser, THE SOUL IN MEAPHYSICAL AND EMPIRICAL PSYCHOLOGY. Pp. X and 275. Price: paper $4.25, cloth $5.00. Published also in German, Dutch, and French.

Volume Eight—Albert Dondeyne, CONTEMPORARY EUROPEAN THOUGHT AND CHRISTIAN FAITH. Pp. XI and 211. Price: paper $5.00, cloth $5.75. Published also in French.

Volume Nine—Maxwell J. Charlesworth, PHILOSOPHY AND LINGUISTIC ANALYSIS. Pp. XIII and 234. Price: paper $4.75, cloth $5.50.

Volume Ten—Remy C. Kwant, PHILOSOPHY OF LABOR. Pp. XI and 163. Price: paper $4.50, cloth $5.25.

Volume Eleven—Remy C. Kwant, ENCOUNTER, Pp. VIII and 85. Price: paper $2.50, cloth $3.25.

In preparation:

William Luijpen, EXISTENTIAL PHENOMENOLOGY.

Andrew G. van Melsen, SCIENCE AND TECHNOLOGY.

P. Henry van Laer, PHILOSOPHY OF SCIENCE. Part Two.

John A. Peters, METAPHYSICS.

CONTENT

FOREWORD

This book contains the lectures which the author delivered as a Visiting Professor in the Graduate School of Duquesne University. The translator is one of his former students, who has followed the publications of Professor Kwant with ever increasing interest. He has always felt that his books and articles—most of them published in Dutch—should be made known to a greater public. It was therefore with great pleasure that he accepted the request to translate the present work into English.

Remy C. Kwant studied traditional scholastic philosophy at the Angelicum in Rome. After a few years of teaching he became thoroughly convinced that philosophy should be an adequate expression of life and, therefore, also of contemporary life. He felt that the evolution of mankind since the Middle Ages required a complete rethinking of our philosophical heritage in the light of modern philosophy.

He went to Paris with the purpose of making an intense study of modern philosophy and particularly of existentialism. He made additional modern studies in Louvain, specializing in the philosophy of Merleau-Ponty. Contacts with scientists made him reflect upon the philosophical principles which underlie modern scientific thought.

This book is actually a discussion of philosophy with Scholastic thinkers, existentialists, scientists, and Marxist philosophers. In this discussion, which is at the same time in part a critical analysis of these four systems, the author is able to throw new light upon the social nature of man. He discovers new perspectives in the realms of metaphysics, ethics, and theology. This book should be of great interest to readers in America, where "Human Relations" have become a new science and where "togetherness" is a nationally discussed topic.

The many footnotes quoting from German, French, and Dutch publications have also been translated. The translator has added all the subtitles and the two indexes at the end of this book.

Acknowledgment is made to Miss Mary M. Mastrianni who was kind enough to read the manuscript and to suggest a few linguistic corrections.

Robert C. Adolfs, O.S.A.

Mechanicville N. Y.,
January 28, 1960.

VIII

INTRODUCTION

History portrays a continuous interaction between society and the individual. It is within a society that the individual comes to maturity. He may think of himself as an independent being, capable of judging the society in which he lives and even condemning it. This is merely an illusion of independence, however, which often makes him forget that he is in reality, at least to a great extent, shaped by his society.

The individual himself also influences society. He develops new ideas and new patterns of behavior, which form the basis of new relationships in his social environment. These new relationships are the state of being-together. Although history *per se* does not always outline progression toward social development, we feel that to-day involvement between the individual and society is an ever deepening process of interaction.

At the beginning of our modern age we find an extreme form of individualism. The philosopher imagined himself to be independent and self-reliant in his thinking. The intellect was enlightened, he thought, by clear and distinct ideas or by meaningful impressions, none of which included the social state, man's being-together. In the manuals of the late-scholastic era one reads, without any reference to man's social being, that the first self-evident principles of the theoretical intellect and the first principles of morality were given to the individual.[1] Religion was described as the road to personal salvation and ascetical treatises emphasized self-sanctification. Some even claimed that society came into being through a decision of free individuals. Nowhere do we find such individualistic thinking and living as in the last century.

Precisely in this same period we also see the growth of a powerful apparatus of production. The industrial revolution was uniting mankind more than ever in a labor order. In this same period of extreme individualism, Marx could write about the socializing power of labor and foresee the world of the future, although not without certain exaggerations.

---

[1] "Lex naturalis est conceptio seu cognitio in actu secundo; dicitur naturaliter indita; non quasi ipsa cognitio, sive in actu secundo sive in actu primo (idea), sit innata, sed quia innata est homini inclinatio et facilitas statim, ubi primum rationis usus evigilat, abstrahendi ex sensibilibus notiones communissimas ordinis practici (ut est notio boni et mali) et formulandi ex iis principia universalissima ordinis practici." Josephus Gredt, *Elementa philosophiae aristotelico-thomisticae,* Friburgi Brisgoviae, ed. VII, 1937, vol. II, page 348.

Dr. F. A. Weve interprets the Late-Scholastic tradition as follows: "Just as our social character presupposes human nature, and this nature must logically be regarded as prior to this character, so is the experience of the "we" based upon the experience of the "self" as an independent substance and presupposes it." "Staat en algemeen welzijn bij Aristoteles en S. Thomas," *De structuur van staat en gemeenschap (Verslag van de negentiende algemene vergadering van de vereniging voor thomistische wijsbegeerte)*, Utrecht, 1954 page 4 (Reprinted from *De Annalen van het Thijmgenootschap,* vol. 42, no. 3).

Our existence is now, more than ever, a social existence, a being-together. We have captured, so to speak, a new power over nature. This power is in the hands of the group and, therefore, it must be called a social power. The individual participates in the social power by fulfilling a function.

We are becoming aware of the extent and of the depth of our alliance with society through the crises which develop in our lives and in our thinking. There still remain vestiges of exaggerated individualism when people resist the integration of their lives into society and look with reluctance and reservation upon the social structure of our existence.

This book is written to show the extent to which our existence is involved in a state of being-together. The author holds the view that human involvement in the state of being-together gives full meaning and significance to all things, even to matter. This new perspective compels us to rethink our sciences, metaphysics, and ethics. In this book a number of vistas are opened up without being fully developed. For the author himself, they meant a deepening of his philosophical attitude. It is his hope that this may be the case also for some of his readers.

CHAPTER ONE

KNOWLEDGE OF THINGS AND KNOWLEDGE OF MAN

1. *Fundamental Questions*

When we reflect on our knowledge of things and of man, we observe that an opposition exists between the two. To a certain extent we are familiar with both objects of cognition. We are familiar with the things we use daily: table, chair, pen and paper, tools, and raw materials. We are familiar also with our relatives, friends, and the people we meet regularly. But perceptiveness is not reciprocal between things and man. We know a thing, but a thing does not recognize us. It is unable to look at us, to see us, to judge us. We do not look at a thing for sympathy and pity. It cannot give us an answer to our questions. It is used by us without having a will of its own. Of course, we have to take into account the nature of a thing; we cannot smoke a pencil or write with a cigar. But a thing is unable to protest when we use it wrongly. At most we are in danger of causing undesirable effects, but this does not mean that the thing is indignant and turns against us.

This description of a thing is negative. We can describe a thing best only by indicating what it is not and does not have; it is not and does not have what a person is and has. If we want to characterize a thing positively, we are faced with a real problem. On the one hand, we do know what a thing is but, on the other, we cannot put it into words. The reason for this is, that the idea "thing" is one of our most fundamental ideas, and we are therefore unable to describe it further. Describing it would require more fundamental ideas and we do not have ideas beyond the most fundamental ones.

Nevertheless, we are capable of indicating a few properties which pertain to a thing precisely insofar as it is a thing. No one, for example, doubts that he would sink if he tried to walk on water. We know that a well-constructed bridge will support us when we cross it. We thus depend upon things because we are sure of their functions. If a thing reacts differently from what is expected, we investigate because we are sure that an explanation is possible. If salt is really salt, it will give a certain flavor to food. We may put permanent properties into laws and these laws are immutable.

The impressive descriptions of a "thing" which we find in the work of Sartre are all negative. He describes *thing* as complete darkness, as something which "lies crushed on itself."[1] This description, however, is negative, for it merely indicates that a thing is not a person. Accordingly, although we are capable of saying something positive about a thing,

---

[1]   Cf. Jean-Paul Sartre, *L'être et le néant, Essai d'ontologie phénoménologique,* Gallimard, Paris, 1943, pages 30-34.

when we really want to be clear we resort to negatieve descriptions.[2]
It is as if we are really better acquainted with persons than with things.
We are familiar with persons, with ourselves. Often, for instance, we
use the word "I." We mix socially with other people every day, and
although we may have problems in our dealings with people, we cannot
say that our everyday associations with them are always full of problems.

These reflections imply a fundamental question: what is more
familiar to us, things or people? Another question pertains to a possible
connection between these two ways of cognition. Do we reach people
through things or is it possible that we become familiar with things
through people? So far this question has not been asked very often. But
closer reflection makes us realize the importance of this question and
the extent to which the answer throws light on many philosophical
problems. In order to understand and to become aware of the importance
of our question, we must look into the history of thought about man.
Without making any attempt to be complete, let us look at certain
thoughts of psychology and some philosophical forms of materialism.

2. *The Hypothesis of the Primacy of Thing-Knowledge*

From the analytic point of view, the first thing that strikes us in the
relatively short history of psychology is the tendency to approach man
in a thing-like fashion. Using the methods of the empirical sciences,
some forms of psychology have treated man in the same way as these
sciences treat their non-human objects.

A. *Psychology of Consciousness*

The first representative of this empirical approach to man is *Wundt*,
who is responsible to a great extent for the psychology of consciousness.[3]
The name of this science justifies the assumption that this is an
investigation of what is proper to the person. Psychology of consciousness
is based on the assumption of Descartes that we should draw a sharp

---

[2]   Maurice Merleau-Ponty gives an elaborate description of the "thing" in his
Phénoménologie de la perception, Gallimard, Paris, 1945, pages 366-377. From
the very beginning Sartre sets consciousness and thing in opposition to each
other; Merleau-Ponty, on the other hand, begins his explanation with a description
of the co-existence of our consciousness with the "thing." "We understand the
'thing' as we understand a new behavior, that is, not by an intellectual classification but by recapturing in our minds the way of existence such as it is outlined by
observable signs" (page 369). But he also recognizes the fundamental strangeness
which the "thing" possesses: "The 'thing' ignores us, it rests in itself. We will see
it, if we lay aside our occupations and approach it with a metaphysical and
disinterested attention. It is then hostile and strange" (page 372). He tries to
solve the inherent contradiction of these two aspects by, what he calls, "a logic
of the world, which my entire body appropriates" (page 377). Because of the
openness of my perceptive experience, I can coexist with what is strange to me.
[3]   Wundt's general views may be studied in any standard work on psychology.

line between two main areas of experience; the interior and the exterior. The latter belongs to the physical order, the former to the psychological. In the physical order we come upon phenomena which are obscure and not aware of themselves. But in the order of the psyche, we find conscious phenomena. We sense here the sharp distinctions between what is personal and what is a "thing." Two cognitive modes correspond to these two areas of experience. We have an exterior knowledge about the physical. The area of consciousness requires an interior reflection, self-observation, introspection. Consequently, we would expect that the conscious, the personal, in such a psychology would not be approached in a thing-like fashion.

We are disappointed, however, in this expectation. Wundt intends to analyze the basic elements of our psychic life. He distinguishes between two classes of elements—namely, elementary perceptions and simple feelings. Colors and forms are elements of perception for the eyes. Every outer sense has its own elements of perception. The experience of concrete things is a composition of these elements. Naturally the question arises how we make a whole, how we compose these elements of perception. Wundt explains this through the sense of association.

While all this is very interesting, it does not satisfy us. Reflecting on our field of perception, should we not say that our first experience is a perception of the thing, of the whole? Standing before the painting of a modern artist, whose work I do not understand, I may say that I do not perceive anything. Certainly, I see many lines and colored squares, but I do not really have a perception in the true sense of the word, because I do not see a whole. And as long as I do not discover the whole I have a feeling of strangeness.[4] I sometimes do not even see the elements when I perceive the whole. In other words, it is possible for me to observe a thing without knowing the composing elements. A face is not for me a combination of eyes, nose, mouth and cheeks. The more recent Gestalt psychology claims therefore correctly that in perceptions we do not progress from the parts to the whole but vice versa.

The important question here is, how did Wundt—not because of, but in spite of the testimony of experience— arrive at his opinion? He must have had some reason for his viewpoint. The explanation is found in the methods of the natural sciences, which have the physical world as their exclusive object. The purpose of these sciences is to study the component parts of the whole and to understand the whole through

---

[4] Merleau-Ponty emphasizes that there is true perception only if I pry into the totality of the "thing" which manifests itself in all its forms of appearance. "The unity of the 'thing' beyond all its fixed properties is not a substratum, an empty X, a subject of inherence; it is that unique accentuation which is found in each individual thing, that unique manner of existence of which these properties are only a secondary expression." *Phénoménologie de la perception,* page 368. Thus I understand a work of art only if I see all its details in the light of its unity.

the study of its parts. Through observation and classification of many facts, scientists try to establish general laws which explain the whole. We do not go too far if we suspect that Wundt was influenced by this methodology. True, he distinguishes the physical from the conscious but, on the other hand, he approaches consciousness methodologically as something physical. Implicitly he acknowledges the primacy of thing-knowledge.

B. Behaviorism

This trend becomes even more evident in the psychological system of behaviorism.[5] This system originated as a reaction against the fact that psychology was not sufficiently scientific. True science, the behaviorists said, should be based on facts that are observable by all. They maintained that all that takes place in the inner self of man, in his consciousness, is observable only by the one who experiences it. Therefore, they said, this cannot be an object of science. Only the outward behavior of man is observable to all, and only this can be an object of scientific reflection for the psychologist. The rest belongs to the domain of the novelist. The observed behavior consists of many stages between which there is apparently some connection. Given that behavior is always a reaction to stimuli, the behaviorists conclude that the purpose of scientific psychology is to discover laws governing the connection of stimuli and behavior, and the stages of behavior. Man is here obviously approached as a "thing." Actually they no longer even want to speak of the person. This type of psychology reduces the person to nothing more than a mechanism of behavior. According to the behaviorist Watson, that is all that man is.

Implicitly or openly these psychologies commit themselves to the primacy of thing-knowledge. Scientific research concerns itself more frequently with things, because things offer the best basis for exact and precise knowledge. Whatever is not approachable in a thing-like fashion is either distrusted or denied. Even if it did exist, they hold, it would be irrelevant as an object of science.

C. The Approach of Materialism

In philosophy also we find clear traces of such viewpoints. In his inaugural address "A Gentle Force," Dr. Linschoten has convincingly demonstrated that the above-mentioned forms of psychology have a

---

[5] A critical commentary on behaviorism from the viewpoint of phenomenology may be found in Merleau-Ponty, *La structure du comportement,* nouvelle édition précédée de *Une philosophie de l'ambiguité* par Alphonse de Waelhens, Paris, 1949, Ch. I, Le comportement réflexe, pages 5-54.

philosophical background.[6] *Locke* already said that our cognitive life is made up of primitive elements, and he pointed to association as the active power which constructs wholes from elements. Association is indeed to him a sort of power.[7] *Hobbes* thought of the psychic life as a mechanical whole. We respond to a stimulus by perceiving, as water responds to cold by freezing. Here again, these philosophers see the human being from the thing-like point of view. To think of personal, "live" processes in a thing-like fashion is characteristic of any form of materialism.

In this connection *Marxism* denotes two levels in the social life of man, a lower and an upper level. The lower level is made up of labor, the industrial-economic sector of human life, in one word, the ways in which people work together to cultivate the earth. The upper level consists of the other aspects of being-together: philosophy, religion, art and literature. Marxism teaches that the upper level is *determined* by the lower.[8] The upper level is a *necessary* mirror-like reflection of the economic-industrial structure. This is again a thing-like relationship, because it is proper to things to have necessary relations. It is also characteristic of Marxism that personal, subjective intentions are discounted in its consideration of man. One who is the owner or manager of a factory belongs to the capitalistic class and, as such, is evil. He may be a good, noble man and very socially inclined; he may spend most of his profits on social benefits. All that does not count. He is a capitalist and consequently evil and wrong.

Extreme *evolutionism*—another form of materialism—bases itself on the same kind of thinking. Man is viewed as a sort of higher *thing*, the result of a long, thing-like, process of development.

---

[6] "The association theory is the theory of 'the mechanical man'; this theory never *concluded* that what happens in the psyche is mechanical, but it stated this *a priori,* inspired by the fundamental Cartesian concept of man... This assumption, that to explain psychic happenings is to reduce them to physiological processes which function mechanically, leads to the remarkable consequence that psychology should occupy itself exclusively with physico-chemical processes." J. Linschoten, *A gentle force, beschouwingen over het associatiebegrip,* Groningen, 1957, page 18.

[7] "What could not happen to an investigator who is tracing footprints, has happened to the psychologist; he forgot that the footprints were made by someone and now thinks that his job consists in studying the gravel." *Ibid.,* page 23.

[8] "The general result, which has guided me in my further studies, may be summarized in the following way. Men make their own lives in a social way. In doing so, they enter into relations which are necessary and do not depend on their own free will. These relations are production relations. They correspond to the phase of evolution of the material means of production. The whole of the production relations constitutes the economic conditions of society. They are the real basis of life. On this basis men build a juridical and political structure, and to these structures corresponds a way of thinking. The method of production conditions social, political, and spiritual life. It is not man's way of thinking which determines his being but man's social being which determines his way of thinking." Karl Marx, *Zur Kritik der politischen Ökonomie,* Dietz Verlag, Berlin, 1951, Vorwort, p. 13.

D. *The Primacy of Thing-Knowledge According to the "Natural Attitude"*

Our initial question was about the knowledge of things and people. We wondered which knowledge should be given primacy. It appears now, that in modern thinking, be it psychology or philosophy, there exists a tendency to confer this primacy upon the knowledge of things and to approach the human person in the same thing-like manner. This trend of modern thought has an underlying presumption—namely, that things have greater intelligibility than the human person. But, we may ask, is this really the case?

We noted at the outset of this chapter that in an attempt to describe a "thing" we often resort to a negative description, a denial of everything situated in the domain of personal existence. The tendency, then, to confer primacy on thing-knowledge demands further explanation.

One possible approach to the problem may be found in Husserl's theory of "natural attitude" (*natürliche Einstellung*). In the spirit of this theory we could say that we are apparently living in a clear and transparent world of things. We know what everything in our environment is and what purpose it has. The world around us seems to hide hardly any secrets. When I observe the things in my room or look out of the window at the street and the buildings outside, I am in a familiar world. Certainly there are some things with which I am not familiar. It is possible that I may not know how to drive a car, how to operate a complicated machine. But this ignorance is merely factual. In principle, I could know how to drive by learning how to drive, by mastering the mechanics of driving. I could learn how to operate a machine, any complicated machine. "Directions for Use" are so to speak, engraved on things. No wonder that one hears from time to time about man's progressive lack of imagination. Everything in our every day environment has such a clear intelligibility, that there seems to be hardly any room for mysteries. In principle, we are able to master the mechanism of any complicated thing and we have consequently no fear of it, since it has a clear function, a clear meaning.

I was told by a man who spent some time in Africa that the white man who dares to enter the African wilderness often shows fear, and that the natives who are accustomed to the jungle look down upon him and scorn him for it. It is understandable that the white man should show fear when he is among such strange and weirdly unfamiliar things. In our own world we go about relaxed and at ease. Meaning and use are fixed and determined either by the nature of the things or the use given to them through construction. For this reason our world is not free from a certain monotony. In things themselves there are many hidden possibilities, some of which we may have realized, and others which we may have suppressed. This too, may account for the blindness of modern man for symbols. He sees the established meaning of things and cannot easily see the symbolic.

8

It is precisely in this realm that things are perceived as wholes composed of parts, and that one is able to understand things because of their component elements. The walls of our buildings consist of brick and mortar, steel and concrete. To know something means to know of what it is composed, how it is constructed, how it is put together. It is true that the parts are made for the intended whole. But after the whole is finished, one can take it apart again and rebuild it without having a fundamental change. Homes have been constructed in such a way that they can be taken apart and put together again at some other spot. A great clarity and intelligibility indeed prevails here and not for modern man only. Experiments show that primitive people also who only recently entered the civilized world, quickly learn to live in this clear and intelligible world of ours.

We may pause here to note that clearness is closely related to the ease of learning the mechanics of things and ease in manipulating them. Things are becoming increasingly easier to manipulate. A good example is the driving of a car. Twenty-five years ago driving required considerable and complicated manipulations. Modern mechanisms, such as push-button transmission, power-brakes, and power-steering manifest the progress made towards greater maneuverability and intelligibility. In terms of the huge mechanized tools which we possess, we may say that our world consists of manipulatable things, and this holds for the macrocosmos as well as the microcosmic world.[9] Once again, therefore, it appears to be true that within this world things are more familiar to us than are people.

This seems to become even more evident if we consider man as a factor in industrial production. Raw materials, machines and manpower are the main factors in a production process. If there are any troubles in this process, man is frequently the cause. Laborers have greater or lesser zest for work; unknown factors may slown down their activity; they may put forth demands and go out on strike. Unpredictable factors influence the output and quality of their work. While natural sciences tell us how to manipulate matter, other sciences, such as psychology and sociology of labor, show us how to manipulate man. There is no doubt about the fact that the natural sciences are far more succesful than the sociological sciences. Man remains the Great Unknown. Scientists may sometimes think that they have finally caught him in a system of laws, but in the end they have to admit that man escapes all systematization. Economic calculations sometimes also failed because man proved to be an incalculable factor. This is preeminently true of our modern society and to a certain extent of every society.

Summarizing, we may say that it seems to be an agreeable and

---

[9] "This world is for me not only a world of things, but just as immediately the world of values, the world of goods, and the practical world." Edmund Husserl, *Ideen zu einer reinen Phänomenologie und phänomenologischen Philosophie,* erstes Buch, *Husserliana* III, The Hague 1950, page 59.

acceptable truth, founded on physical reality and conventional philosophical and psychological thinking, that we are more familiar with things than with man.

3. *The Illusion of the Naturalness of Our Familiar World of Things*

The phenomenological analysis of the "natural attitude" saves us from hasty conclusions. The "natural attitude" is a tendency of our thinking to consider the actual, self-explanatory, and transparent world as natural and original. Aware of this danger, we may ask if the above description of a great intelligible world of things is truly original.

The answer to this question must be in the negative. Our familiar world is a cultured world, in which we do not come upon things in their primitive and original undisturbedness. The world of materials and appliances is a cultural datum, pointing to culturally creative man; it is a datum already permeated by our creative presence.

Our familiarity with the things that surround us comes to us through our familiarity with our fellow men. This familiarity exists only for one who knows how to behave in a certain way. It has no absolute character, but is coherent with a pattern of behavior which we have learned from the society in which we were brought up. A native from te jungle, suddenly transferred to our environment, would not be familiar at all with the things in our world. Interhuman communication has made our environment something which appears quite natural and obvious to us.

The world, however, does not consist only of utensils and implements. We are capable also of looking at this world with an objective interest or with a glance of admiration. These are the ways in which the scientist or the artist approaches the world. In these spheres also there exist things that are known. There also one could suspect that the person is less known and more mysterious to us than are things. Science, for example, can handle things much more easily than persons. In our time physical science is in possession of its method of approach. Psychology, on the other hand, appears to be still searching for its approach—at least, periodically a new method is proposed to replace its predecessors.

Nevertheless, a closer inspection reveals here also that the opposite is true. First of all, we are not born with this theoretical outlook and this esthetic attitude. They are the fruit of a long history.[10] Man had to discover these approaches as possibilities contained in his mode of being, and this discovery demanded an extended period of self-development. Thus the attitude itself in which the world becomes a theoretical or esthetic spectacle is something which arises in the course of history. Although the attitude must, of course, be given as a hidden possibility of man, this does not mean that its development cannot be historically determined.

---

[10] Husserl elaborates this in the first chapter of the second volume of his above-mentioned book. See *Husserliana IV,* pages 1-27.

Secondly, the world of theory depends upon the existence of language, and language is a social possession. In the past, its importance for thought has been ignored. There is the old distinction between thing, concept, and word(name). Too long the connection between the name and the thing named has been disregarded, as though a name were something incidental. For realistic philosophers a thing was supposed to be completely independent of the concept, and the concept independent of the word (or name).

But should we not, on the other hand, in analyzing the cognitive process, note that there is first of all a vague, undifferentiated area of perception?[11] In perceiving a whole, the individual elements do not stand out. They are absorbed, so to speak, in the whole, and no sharp outlines are visible. Let us take, for example, the man who enters a museum, knowing nothing about art. He sees everything and yet, he sees nothing. Another example is the little child, who has the same area of perception as his parents in the same room. But most of the things in the room are meaningless for the small child. He sees everything and still hardly anything. Individual things emerge and become meaningful through words. *Words bring things to light.* According to Merleau-Ponty, to know the world means to sing of it in a melody of words.[12] We learn how to use words for things through intersubjective communication. In doing so, we approach things in a *new* way, and they begin to exist for us in a new clearness. The word indeed presupposes the thing, but we may say that to name a thing does not leave the thing undisturbed altogether.

All this becomes more evident if we pose the question: what does it mean for us to say that a science exists? It does not simply signify the existence of the object of this science. As long as our physical world has been in existence, its elements, its atoms and its molecules have also existed. In other words, the structure of matter existed already, it did not have to wait for the discovery of the scientist to become existent. Science, therefore, is not the existence of a thing. It is rather *a particular way in which man regards the world*; it is consequently a particular way of naming things. This way of naming things existed in the mind of the scientist and later on was recorded in books. One who wishes to be a scientist has to acquire this particular way of naming things, and so he may arrive at scientific understanding. This way of naming things does not leave the things entirely undisturbed. It brings things to light; the way in which things come to light is connected with the way we speak about them. It is evident from these considerations that the scientific realm is in some way associated with mutual contacts

---

[11] Cf. Jean-Yves Calvez, *La pensée de Karl Marx,* Paris 1956, pages 354-359.

[12] "I say that *I know an idea,* whenever I have the ability to organize around it reflections which have a coherent meaning." Maurice Merleau-Ponty, "Sur la phénoménologie du language," *Problèmes actuels de la phénoménologie,* Paris, 1952, page 101.

11

among people. The theoretical realm of the natural sciences really begins to exist for me, when I acquire a particular way of thinking and speaking (including, of course, understanding). Both are results of intersubjective communication.

4. *The Primary Role of Interhuman Communication*

We have reflected upon two clear worlds of things: manipulatable things and things which are the object of scientific thinking. In both cases we might have thought that this clearness existed for us independently of our interhuman relations. In both cases conventional thinking might have led us to believe that the world of things had a privileged clarity over and above the intersubjective encounter. But we have seen that the opposite is true: we attain the clearness of things through intersubjective communication.

What, then, created the illusion that the realm of things has greater clarity? This happened because we accepted the clear world of things as a conventional datum, without reflecting upon the way in which we arrived at this clearness. But reflecting upon it, we had no difficulty in discovering that interhuman relations are a mediating factor in our knowledge about things. These considerations lead to a certain hypothesis: might it be possible that not things but our fellow men are primary reality for us? Is it not through interhuman relations that we, epistemologically speaking, arrive at things?

The affirmative reply is a philosophical hypothesis. It is one of the many possible answers to the question of our primary knowledge. This question, however, is not concerned with what we knew at the moment when our cognitive life began. The reply to the last-named question is hidden in impenetrable darkness, because the child is unable to inform us about it when his cognitive life begins and later we ourselves cannot recall it. The question of our primary knowledge has therefore some other meaning.

Our cognitive life is rich and manifold. The philosopher's task is to bring unity into this multiplicity. That is the reason why it is so important for him to detect what is first and above all known to us. Having established this, he will be able to lay out the structure of our cognitive life. Every important philosophy has its own view on this point, and this view is decisive for epistemology, metaphysics, and anthropology. It is decisive for epistemology, because it clarifies the structure of knowledge. Besides, all the possibilities of knowing are contained in its beginning. It is decisive for metaphysics, because it is in and through our knowledge that we view "being." The primitive way in which we perceive reality answers the question to what extent "being" is accessible to us. It is decisive also for anthropology, because knowledge is one of man's essential aspects. The very view taken of human knowledge contains a conception of man.

We would like therefore to investigate whether the factor of inter-human communication is perhaps the most primordial and fundamental form of knowledge. This will be the case if this knowledge itself is not reducible to something else, and if all other knowledge depends on it. The truth and the importance of this hypothesis will grow evident as we proceed.

CHAPTER TWO

THE PRIMORDIAL AND IRREDUCIBLE NATURE
OF INTERSUBJECTIVE CONTACT

We have explained in the first chapter that there have been scientists who attributed primacy to our knowledge of things. We have tried to explain this viewpoint as follows: if we reflect on our cognitive life as it appears at first glance, it seems obvious that we should attribute primacy to the knowledge of things. To all appearance there is greater clarity and intelligibility in the world of functional objects and in the sphere of scientific study which deals with things. If we place ourselves within this clearness, the human being becomes very mysterious and we are inclined to think that man is not more familiar to us than things. But deeper reflection showed that in reality we become familiar with things *through* interhuman relations. It is only through the encounter with others that we really get to know things. The greater intelligibility of things, therefore, appears to be a superficial illusion.

1. *Attempts to Reduce the Knowledge of Man to Thing-Knowledge*

Those who accepted the primacy of things attempted to answer the question of the way in which we acquire knowledge about man. Thing-knowledge was something self-evident for them, whereas of man knowledge appeared to be perplexing. For these philosophers it was therefore almost a natural thing to start from thing-knowledge in order to gain knowledge about the human person. In other words, they tried to reduce the knowledge of man to the knowledge of things. We will attempt to follow this line of thought, but as we will see, the forced and spasmodic character of this way of thinking will compel us to acknowledge the irreducible nature of our knowledge of man.[1]

In his cognitive situation, they said, man faces a world of phenomena. There are two poles in our knowledge, a subjective pole and an objective pole. The subjective pole is the experiencing "ego," which we co-experience in all knowledge, since our knowledge is conscious of itself; the objective pole is the world of phenomenal reality, which does not include the other's personality. Just as the knowing "ego" is an interior reality, so the "you" of the other man—if it really exists—is an interiority and, consequently, does not appear in the objective world. It is not a phenomenon among phenomena, for the world of phenomena has a thing-like nature. In this world of phenomena, however, I observe realities which I specify as other persons, which I address as "you" and of which I speak as "him." The problem arises therefore, how did I arrive at this way of acting?

---

[1] Much valuable information concerning this subject matter may be found in an article of F. J. J. Buytendijk, "Persoon en Ontmoeting," *Tijdschrift voor strafrecht,* vol. 62, no. 3, 1954, pages 193-207.

First of all we must ask ourselves, what exactly do we observe when we focus our attention on other people? We observe certain forms of behavior. We see a body moving, eyes focused on us, we hear the person speaking, and we see the motions of his hand emphasizing what he is trying to express. Briefly, we see a pattern of behavior unfolding before our eyes. But we do not see the inner person. The actual "you" remains hidden from us. Still, we do speak about it.

There is, however, so they claim, a road that leads into the "you" of the other man, because it is not true that I know myself only through inner experience. I also know myself in as far as I manifest myself outwardly. I can analyze myself, when I am acting outwardly in the world. In that case I speak of an exterior manifestation of my personality. I do know my exterior behavior as a manifestation of my inner self. I know for example, that my reaching for food corresponds to inner feelings of hunger, that my speaking originates from evidence which has been innerly experienced, that my absent-mindedness may be the result of boredom. Noting the same behavior in other people, I am inclined to conclude that it is a manifestation also of the other people's inner self. Just as behind my behavior there stands an "I," in the same way there must be a "you" behind the behavior of the other person. Thus I have found an entrance into the inner self of another human being. I recognize my own observed behavior as a manifestation of an interior life and through this behavior I may now penetrate into the inner self of the other person.

Rationalism calls it an illusion to say that we know other people spontaneously and directly. In reality, they say, a complicated cognitive process is behind this seeming spontaneity. But because I am used to this cognitive process, the different stages through which it was developed remain hidden from me. An example will demonstrate that this happens all the time. When I am playing cards, and I notice that the other player has all the aces and kings five times in a row, I know that there is something peculiar in this situation. I know it because in an ordinary situation where no regularity can be expected, I do observe an obvious regularity, and unconsciously I apply the rule that all regularity has a cause. When I accuse the player of fraud, I am absolutely sure, but I am not aware of the different stages of my reasoning. The same holds also in our problem. I know the other person through a rather complicated process of reasoning, but the phases of its development escape me. This is the way in which rationalism tries to explain how we attain knowledge about other people by unconsciously applying rational principles from the world of things.

2. *The Erroneous Assumptions of This Explanation*

The above explanation may appear to be very logical, but does not agree with the facts. In the first place, it is assumed here that self-experience always plays a role in man's knowledge of other people. But if we look at the behavior of little children, for example, we doubt very much that this assumption agrees with reality. Children, even very little children, who certainly have no introspection, are very sensitive to the facial expressions of adults, even to very small nuances of it. They react differently to a friendly or angry face. They seem to sense the mood of the mother who bends over them. The child may approach his father and his mother in different ways, and he knows to choose the right moment for asking something. He knows even the weaker moments in the parents' feelings. It is unthinkable that the child knows everything about the parents' inner feelings through self-experience.

Moreover, we know other people not only as resembling our own inner self, but also as being different from us. We are able, therefore, to enter to a certain extent into a person's feelings in situations which we ourselves have never experienced. This would be impossible if self-experience were the only key to the door of the mysterious inner life of other people.

A second assumption seems to be that I within myself would distinguish between inner experience and its outward manifestation, that I would know both separately and would be aware of the connection between them. This again is not in agreement with reality. The interior experience and its outward manifestation are so intermingled that a comparison of the two is inconceivable. If I am overcome with great joy, it will manifest itself in my facial expression, in my way of speaking, or even in my gestures. Feelings of joy and their outward expressions are interwoven. We do not mean that they are completely identical. That this is not the case is evidenced by the fact that man, to a certain extent, can control the expression of his feelings. But even where the distinction is clear, the intermingling is also apparent. Whoever controls the outward manifestation of joy, tempers his joy and, at the same time, drives it into the background of his emotional life. The outward manifestations are spontaneous extensions of our inner life. It seems as if the inner life comes into existence in its exterior manifestation. When expressions of joy are suppressed by a compelling force, joy itself dies.

The above-mentioned way of thinking would have us believe that we look from our inner self at its manifestations. But in reality, through our manifestations, we experience the world in a particular fashion. Frequently we do not even know our outward behavior or, at any rate, other people seem to know it better that we do ourselves. The outward manifestations belong to our nature. Therefore it is unrealistic to think that one could penetrate into the inner self of someone else by making a comparison of outward manifestations. Such a comparison seems to be a rational construction which does not correspond with reality. All this is very evident if we consider the so-called "character." A "character" is someone who behaves in a very peculiar way, which is characteristic of himself only. But he is a true "character" only if he is not aware of being one. A person deliberately behaving in a peculiar way is a poseur, not a character. A "character" does not know that he behaves peculiarly; his conduct is interwoven with his personality.

The several stages which, according to the rationalistic viewpoint, were supposed to explain the understanding of our fellow man now appear to be imaginary. In general, the spontaneity of interhuman relations excludes discursive reasoning. To illustrate, let us think for a moment of children in a room who are being entertained by a clever story-teller, one who knows how to captivate his audience. By watching them we may see on their faces a rich variety of moods. Assuming that these children apply unconsciously a number of complicated rational principles is an absurdity.

3. *The Knowledge of Man Has no Intermediary, but is Direct and Spontaneous*

The line of approach stated at the beginning of this chapter proved to be wrong. This approach assumed that the interpretation of outward manifestations was the key to understanding the inner self of man. Now it appears that the way this problem was posed is false. The human person is not concealed *behind* his outward behavior, but exists *in it*. It was originally assumed that the self is invisible, but now we see that he is *existence*, he is being-in-the-world. The human personality is not hidden by the body as by a veil; his outward behavior is the *embodiment* of the inner self. He exists and appears in the body and is directly accessible to us. When we use expressions such as, "*See* how happy he is," "*See* how bored they are," "*Look* how angry she is," we must take these words literally. Grief and joy, anger and meekness, love and hatred are *themselves* visible, observable.

We would like to make our assertions clear by answering three objections that could be made. The most essential phenomena of personal life are undoubtedly *thinking* and *freedom*. Are not these phenomena hidden and do they not escape observation? There is furthermore the fact that man can hide his personality by *deception*. All this seems to contradict our thesis that knowledge of man is direct and immediate.

A. First Objection: Man's Thinking

The primordial and most primitive form of thinking is not found in thinking-put-into-words, but in behavior. Behavior is a complex process, which is truly human only if its many phases have inner coherence.

18

We are not referring to physical reflexes when we speak of human behavior. We are referring to those patterns of behavior which have been contrived by man. When we say "contrived by man," we do not mean one particular human individual. We adopt patterns of behavior from the society in which we live. But we do so in a human way only if we adopt *with understanding*. Human behavior embodies genuine understanding. This understanding becomes manifest in behavior itself. The inner coherence itself of a behavior pattern, the logical harmony of its various phases, is a result of thinking. It would be wrong to believe that this thinking precedes the behavior and that the latter is pure execution. On the contrary, thinking consists *in the behavior itself*.

Let us consider the simple example of a mother involved in the hygienic care of her baby. This is a meaningful and coherent activity. Many things are used, a little tub, warm water, soap, powder, towels etc. They are used in a meaningful succession of quickly executed acts. Everything is concentrated around the little body of the child. The mother knows her job and handles it intelligently. Does that mean that the mother knows in theory what she is doing? Not necessarily. If we asked her to give an explanation of her actions, she probably would not be able to explain the theory. She "knows," but this kind of knowing *exists* in her behavior and does not precede it. Man "thinks" with his hands, with the movements of his body, in one word, through his behavior. This is the reason why we are not only able to talk foolishly, but also "to act foolishly," the latter meaning the absence of intelligence in our behavior.

The manifestation of intelligence in human activity is very evident in the practice of any fast-moving sport. For example, the way in which a football player takes his position, handles the ball, takes in a situation at a glance and passes the ball, all this is intelligent behavior. Of course, the player has had some kind of theoretical training, but he "knows" more and better with his legs, with his hands, and with his entire body than he knows in theory. If he has to teach another player how to pass a ball, how to tackle, he prefers to demonstrate rather than to give a theoretical explanation. He adjusts the entire posture of his body to the approaching ball, without knowing in theory how all this comes about. There is a genuine "knowing" with the hands and with the body. This knowing is visible and perceptible, and we understand it immediately.

Certainly, there is also another kind of knowing, namely theoretical knowledge. But that, too, is perceptible, since it exists in word. Language is not just an exterior vestment, but an embodiment of thought. The latter cannot exist without some kind of embodiment. It is true, we can think inwardly, but this thinking also utilizes words, as we know from experience. It is the so-called inner or mental word, which is derived from the external word. We may therefore say that embodied thought is perceptible in principle, although not always in actuality, because we sometimes use words without speaking them externally.

Thus thought is in principle perceptible and accessible. We must abandon the Cartesian illusion that thought is something essentially interior and inaccessible, and that communication through words is a secondary and accidental phenomenon. We understand *immediately* the thought which is embodied in behavior and word. Man must learn to understand other people, but this development can take place only within a fundamental understanding that is already present. The intelligibility of another man's thought is always presupposed. We might increase the degree of understanding, but understanding is present from the beginning.

B. Second Objection: Man's Freedom

Our problem seems much more difficult if we focus our attention on human freedom. Many books have been written about the perception of freedom in man. If we assume that freedom, because of its interior nature, is recognizable only through outward behavior, we are faced with a problem for which there is no solution. If we put the actions of man and those of animals on the same level, in order to determine the idea of freedom from a comparison of these phenomena, we will get nowhere. No statistical research based on external behavior will ever establish the fact of freedom. Certainly there is less fixedness and less regularity in human behavior, but this could also be explained by hidden determining factors not yet known to science. The rule applies here, too: freedom is either directly perceptible or we never know it, at least not with certitude.

Experience reveals another man's freedom to us immediately, provided we take experience here as a whole and do not limit it because we have been influenced by certain theories. Let us look at our everyday being-together. We are grateful to one another, we expect certain things from one another; we ask questions of one another; we request that something be done or left alone; we hurt one another, we become offended; we may feel a deep joy, because someone has been very thoughtful to us. This is the social conduct which precedes reflection; we cannot imagine society without it. Even the most primitive people experience this inter-human behavior; no long process of civilization is required to attain it. Even a little child identifies himself very soon with a society and does not have to learn behavior; he reacts spontaneously. This kind of social interaction, however, presupposes freedom and is an absurdity without freedom. One is grateful for a gift, a word, a gesture only because they originate in freedom. The deep joy of the girl who has received a present from her boy-friend owes its depth to the origin of every gift, which is again freedom. A word can hurt or offend us only because it springs from freedom.

All these forms of social conduct are self-evident to us. They are unthinkable without freedom. Freedom, therefore, also is self-evident to us. Apparently, we perceive one another as being free. It is inconceivable that we would know one another's freedom only through reasoning. The fundamental spontaneity of our free acts shows that the opposite is true. From all this we may conclude that the thinking free self, the "self" of the other, in other words, his whole person, is immediately accessible to us. This agrees with one of the fundamental ideas of existentialism, namely, that man is existence, an "existence-in-the-world." Man exists and appears in his embodiment and that is the reason why he is immediately accessible to us. Our knowledge of the other man cannot be reduced to something else and does not come to us through a medium. Philosophers often speak about the mediating function of the body. This is, however, not a mediation in the strict sense of the word, because the person is not concealed in the body, but appears and becomes manifest in the body.

C. Third Objection: Man's Ability to Deceive

There is a feature which strongly seems to contradict our thesis. Man is apparently able to simulate, to deceive, to pretend. This means that he can hide his personality. There are dishonest and insincere people, and frequently we do not know what to think of a person. What is more, man has often been called a mystery, and justifiably so. Jesus Christ said: "Do not judge, that you may not be judged." Christian philosophers, referring to these words of the Gospel, justly point out that man is a secret, a mystery to himself as well as to others. The deeper stirrings of his heart remain hidden for himself and even more so for others. All this is rather generally accepted, and respect for others is properly emphasized. We should acknowledge the mystery in them.

Even though this is true, it does not contradict our thesis. It would indeed be contradictory if the possibility to hide one's personality were based upon the fact that still another self would be concealed behind the visible actuality. This is implied in the objection. It is implied that the actual person is invisible and inaccessible and reveals himself only through inadequate manifestations which, moreover, are subject to freedom.

But the person is not, according to his entire being, an internal actuality which manifests itself fragmentarily and at will. One who has this opinion would apprehend the person as a thing apart. In reality, the person is an ever-developing possibility to encounter things and people. He is always actualizing himself, but this actualization is always partial and never terminal. The possibilities present in an actual encounter are never all totally realized. Let us imagine a man who is a businessman, a good husband and father, and who is interested in art. While he is with his wife and children, his love is actualized; his business characteristics and his interest in art remain in the state of potentiality.

While conducting business, his business attitudes manifest themselves, but the loving father and the aesthete remain hidden. When he visits a museum, we do not see the business man and the husband.

Man never realizes all his possibilities at once. Certain aspects of his person remain in a condition of virtuality. The deeper possibilities have a chance of becoming actualities only within certain encounters. A philosopher may unfold all his possibilities of thought in a conversation with a certain person but not with others. We might describe the "person" in the words of Bergson as an *"immensité de virtualité,"* as a measureless virtuality. The person, therefore, is not to be identified with his actual existence alone, not because there is more actuality behind this existence, but because the possibilities of actualization are endless. A person lacking in manly firmness in a certain environment may show unexpected courage in other circumstances. We may never judge a person because we should never identify him with what he is in his encounter with us. In his potentiality of being, he may transcend his successive actualizations.

This is also the reason why a person is able to pretend and hide his personality. He has, so far as his actualization is concerned, a certain freedom, although this freedom is never complete. An intelligent person is able to refrain from giving himself during a conversation. He may pretend to be ignorant and incompetent. We should notice, however, that the person who pretends never pretends completely. The revelation of self is never completely false in all its aspects. A clever salesman who tries to sell a defective machine hides something he knows, but at the same time, his cleverness and salesmanship manifest themselves. Untruthfulness, proper to all pretense, always appears within a horizon of truth. If there were not a great deal of sincerity, we would not be deceived by an aspect of insincerity.

Therefore, we may not regard the concealment of the person as being similar to the concealment of a thing, which is hidden by an outer covering. Such a thing *exists* in its entirety; it is complete in its actuality. When the cover is removed, it is completely visible. The concealment of a person is an entirely different matter. A person always actualizes himself partially. It is true that it is always the same person who is appearing in his successive actualizations, but in each of the actualizations another facet of that person becomes manifest. Thus, it is quite possible that there are noble possibilities in a person which have never been realized, because they have never been drawn forth. A young man who seems to be phlegmatic, may turn out to be deeply emotional when he meets the girl who allows him to be himself.

The fact that the person manifests himself in his existence does not alter the fact that he is a mystery. None of his manifestations excludes other hidden possibilities. Therefore, the person does not even know himself, at least not completely. There may be hidden possibilities in himself which have never come to light. When a man dreams of a higher form of self-realization, he always dreams of the conditions or situations which will elicit this realization.

The other person manifests himself to us; we are familiar with this manifestation, we understand it. If we reflect upon our social communications with other people, we note that our understanding of them is rich and manifold. We understand an indignant look, a change in the tone of voice, the emotional meaning of a word; we react to them before we are vividly aware of them. Our sensitivity to the other person goes far beyond our rational knowledge. If we were able to translate all knowledge latent in a conversation into the realm of reason, philosophy would gain tremendously. Knowledge about man as expressed in philosophy seems meager in comparison with what we know spontaneously about man in our every-day togetherness.

The thesis which we want to propose in this book is gaining in clarity. Our field of perception is rich in composition. But our primary familiarity lies in the human person as he manifests himself. The being to which we have the greatest access is indeed the personal being. A valuable indication—not a proof—of the truth of this thesis is the fact that the child and the primitive man also have a strong tendency to personify the impersonal. A little child deals with things and animals as though they were persons; primitive man often regards things as though they were animated. The child and primitive man both tend to draw everything within the realm of the personal. Does this not indicate that man's primary familiarity lies within the realm of the personal?

We have come to the conclusion that our knowledge of other people is primordial and irreducible to any other knowledge. We may call this a primordial familiarity. However, our claim here goes further. We want to maintain that we become familiar with the other realities only within this primordial familiarity. Our contact with other people is not just primordial but is also the force which brings us in touch with things. Any form of familiarity is inconceivable unless we are familiar with our fellow men. We intend to make this idea acceptable in the following chapters.

CHAPTER THREE

FAMILIARITY WITH THE WORLD THROUGH CONTACT WITH OUR FELLOW MEN

The thesis which we are defending is that we are primordially familiar with our fellow men and that we proceed from this primordial familiarity to further knowledge. In this chapter we wish to show that this thesis applies to the knowledge which we have of the world in which we live.

1. The Origin of Our Familiarity with the World

Life would be inconceivable without familiarity with the world. Man is familiar with his home and all the objects in it. He also knows the city or town in which he lives, the environment in which he works. The means of public transportation which take him to work are no problem for him. All human behavior takes place within an environment familiar to him, and his conduct presupposes a number of things, the meaning of which is self-explanatory. When I want to smoke a cigaret, I know the meaning of the little plastic band around the cellophane wrapper of the pack. I know the significance of the loose end of this band. I am familiar with the use of tobacco and with the way a cigaret is smoked. I know how to use a lighter and I use it in such a way that I can light the cigaret without burning my fingers. These simple manipulations presuppose many things with which we are familiar. They presuppose a kind of understanding which is not necessarily, and usually not actually, on a rational level. Many meanings are understood within the sphere of behavior, but frequently people would not be able to give a rational explanation of them.

This is pre-reflective knowledge. The world in which we move about has meaning for us, but this meaning is not reflected upon. When we acquire a new behavior, as for example, when we learn a new manual skill, we must learn to live in a new realm of meaning. If one wants to learn how to play the piano, it is not sufficient for him to learn rationally the construction of this musical instrument. He must know the possibilities of this instrument as well, and must learn how to master it with the movements of his fingers. This is knowledge through human activity, which is behavior.

When we learn a skill, we enter into a new realm of meaning.[1] Sometimes, however, this happens with but little awareness. Without realizing it, we adopt quite a few manners and forms of behavior from other people. Each time we make a new pattern of behavior our own, we become familiar with another part of the world around us, because

---

[1] For the intimate connection of instrument and body cf. Merleau-Ponty, *Phénoménologie de la perception*, pages 177-179.

all genuine human behavior is possible only within the familiar realm where understanding exists for us.

What is the origin of this familiarity? We find many diverse answers to this question. There is a primitive line of thought which does not recognize this as problem, because it considers familiarity with the world as a self-evident datum.[2] It is better to regard this thinking as the absence of an historical awareness rather than as positive judgment. It is an undeveloped reflection which disregards the constituted nature of the world in which we live. This lack of regard for our problem is, therefore, not erroneous but an oversight. It is the primitive acceptance of a self-evident world.

An interesting example may be found in the Bible, in the book of Genesis. Activities such as agriculture and cattle-breeding are projected as beginning at the very cradle of humanity. The sons of Adam are spoken of as being involved in these activities. Thus, a world in which man is occupied with agriculture and cattle-breeding is accepted without comment. Descendants of Cain started to forge iron and play musical instruments. According to Genesis, God gave plants as food to man, and after the Deluge He also made animals provide nourishment for man. Cultural achievements are presented as a gift from God. At the time Genesis was written, it was impossible to see the creative force of time. Thanks to archeology we have penetrated deeply into the past and have taken cognizance of communities of people living in the most primitive conditions. Through it, our familiar world of to-day and its origin have become a source of wonderment and perplexity.

2. *The Answers of Three Philosophies*

Rationalism emphasizes the function of the intellect in an effort to explain the origin of knowledge. It regards man in the first place as a thinking spirit and consequently puts all meaning on a rational level. Rationalism will therefore consider all self-evident meaning as hidden rationality. If we should succeed in developing this hidden rationality, we would gain understanding about this self-evident world of ours. It was thinking, the rationalists claimed, that gave meaning to everything in the course of history. The philosopher understands this hidden thinking and reveals it to us. The spirit which, unconscious of itself, was submerged in history is brought to light by the philosopher. The most gigantic effort to elucidate history in this rationalistic fashion was undertaken by Hegel. He drew the whole of history into the orbit of his philosophical thought. While this was to his credit as a philosopher,

---

[2] "The knowledge, which is at the start or immediately our object, can be nothing else than just that which is immedate knowledge, knowledge of the immediate, of what is. We have, in dealing with it, to proceed, too, in an *immediate* way, to *accept* what is given, not altering anything in it as it is presented before us, and keeping mere apprehension free from conceptual comprehension." Hegel, *The Phenomenology of Mind,* 2nd rev. ed. by J. B. Baille, Macmillan, New York, 1949, p. 149.

he conceived the whole of history as an evolution of thought, and this made his view one-sided.[3]

Marx blamed Hegel for making history "walk on its head." Of one of Hegel's followers, Proudhon, he said: "His history takes place in the hazy realm of the imagination and is highly exalted beyond time and place. In short, this is old Hegelian stuff, this is no history, no profane history, no story of mankind, but it is holy history, history of ideas."[4] Marx claimed that history cannot be explained from the realm of the idea. He wanted to put history back on its feet again. In his opinion, the experience of primitive man is empty. Just by looking, man does not discover any meaning. The meaning of things comes into being when man learns how to use things. When, for instance, he stretches his hand to pick fruit from a tree, a meaning is created. The world acquires fuller meaning in proportion to the degree in which man learns to use it. Thus the picking of the fruit becomes a harbinger of labor. Through labor our familiar and meaningful world comes into being.

Accordingly, man progresses from vacuity to full experience, with labor as the mediating factor. This explains also the Marxian theorem of the two levels in society. The lower level consists of the way in which men together cultivate and use the world. The upper level consists of rational ideas, political organization, morality etc., and is determined by the lower level of society. The idea, "the head," of history, is developed through its "feet," that is, the world of labor. Marx recognized this development as social. The individual by himself can do little or nothing. He is absorbed in a social development. Marx thus conceived history as the unfolding of labor and production.

Merleau-Ponty reflecting on our problem, makes a distinction between two levels of existence: the personal and the pre-personal.[5] In reality, the pre-personal level is absorbed into the personal existence. This pre-personal existence is for Merleau-Ponty *the body,* understood by him as relationship-with-the-world, that is, as a subject. For this reason he speaks time and again of the "ego-body," i.e., embodiment as being

---

[3] *"The goal,* which is Absolute Knowledge or Spirit knowing itself as Spirit, finds its pathway in the recollection of the spiritual forms as they are in themselves and as they accomplish the organization of their spiritual kingdom. Their conservation, looked at from the side of their free existence appearing in the form of contingency, is History; looked at from the side of their intellectually comprehended organization, it is the *Science of the ways in which knowledge appears.* Both together, or History (intellectually) comprehended, form at once the recollection and the Golgotha of Absolute Spirit, the reality, the truth, the certainty of its throne." Hegel, *op. cit.,* p. 808.

[4] Karl Marx, *Brief an Annenkow,* Brussel, December 28, 1946; included in *Das Elend der Philosophie,* Dietz Verlag, Berlin, 1957, page 8.

[5] For a more elaborate study of Merleau-Ponty's viewpoints, see Remy C. Kwant, "De geslotenheid van Merleau-Ponty's wijsbegeerte," *Tijdschrift voor Philosophie,* vol. 19, no. 2, 1957, pages 217-272.

relationship-with-the-world. It is exactly this relationship which gives sense and meaning to the world. There is, consequently, a sphere of meaning, which precedes all conscious choice, and from which we cannot withdraw.

Merleau-Ponty expresses this eminently in the following words: "Outside of myself I cannot find a limit to my freedom. But is there possibly a limit in myself? Indeed, we have to make a distinction between our explicit intentions, for example, my plan to climb those mountains, and the general intentions, which virtually permeate my environment with value. Even if I did not decide to climb those mountains, they still appear big to me, because they are beyond the reach of my body. Even though I had just read *Micromégas,* I would be unable to make those mountains small for me. Beneath myself as a thinking subject (who can put himself at will on the star Sirius or on the surface of the earth) there is, so to speak, a natural self, which does not leave its earthly situation and which constantly contrives absolute valuations. Moreover, the plans which I make as a thinking being are apparently based on it. If I decide to look at the world from Sirius' viewpoint, I still have to resort to my earthly experience in order to do so. I might say that the Alps are a *mole-hill.* In as far as I have hands, feet, a body, a world around me, I have intentions which are not determined by my free decision and which permeate my surroundings with characteristics that are not of my choosing."[6]

Merleau-Ponty, therefore, points out that our personal plans and intentions are rooted in corporal intentions which are given with the structure of the body. There is nothing we can do about them, we have to accept them. For this reason, in my realm of meaning, there is a substratum of meaning which I do not choose. He maintains that the "ego-body" with its corresponding realm of meanings is of the most fundamental importance, if we really wish to understand our world. His principal work, from which we have just quoted, is an effort to penetrate into this depth of meaning in order to extract from it some understanding of life and the world. This view is profound and to a great extent original.

3. *Merits and Defects of These Philosophies*

We have indicated three ways of thinking which promise understanding of our familiar world. Rationalism contends that meaning is identical with reason. Marxism views the meaningful world as one which is developed through man's labor. Merleau-Ponty's existential phenomenology searches for understanding by analyzing the fundamental intentions of the "ego-body." In spite of the contrasts between these three ways of thinking there is also a striking similarity between them.

---

[6] Maurice Merleau-Ponty, *Phénoménologie, de la perception,* page 502.

Although Marx rejects some of Hegel's viewpoints, he has read and re-read his works and often indicates his respect for this philosopher. Merleau-Ponty is profoundly inspired by Marxist philosophy and at one time expressed the opinion that all valuable modern tendencies in philosophy are rooted in Hegel's thinking, and may find one another again only in this common source.[7] It appears therefore that all three philosophies emphasize a valuable aspect, and that their points of view do not exclude one another, provided they are stripped of excesses. But we feel that these three views grow to full advantage only if they are regarded within the mutual human encounter.

It is of course impossible to describe the process by which our world becomes familiar and meaningful at its very origin.[8] Just as the adult person cannot revert to childhood in order to understand the processes of his maturation, neither can civilized man put himself mentally in the position of primitive man, in order to trace the genesis of civilization. Knowledge of the structure of civilization, however, is not necessarily dependent upon knowledge of its origin. We can definitely observe how a child, who starts out with mere possibilities, appropriates the rhythm of life in our civilized world.

Rationalism. It is evident that rationalism correctly attributes to intelligence an important role in the process by which our world becomes meaningful and familiar to us. Rationality is present in every sector of man's world, as, for example, in the process of production, in everyday language, in scientific terminology, in every form of art, in good manners, and in all human behavior required in our society. There is a rational order in all these aspects. Only if a child is intelligent, is he susceptible to this order and able to become familiar with it. This is the truth aspect of rationalism.

Its error consists in not recognizing sufficiently the extent to which rationality is incarnate. A human world is inconceivable without the intermingling of matter and rationality; the rational exists precisely in this intermingling and cannot be separated from its materiality. It is indeed true that history is rational, but that does not mean that it is merely a developing process of abstract ideas.

Marx. For this reason Marx was right when he protested against the rationalistic view of history. But by denoting the idea as the "head" and labor as the "feet" of history, he used an image with dangerous implications. Making a distinction between head and feet may easily become a separation, thus turning rationality into an accompanying

---

[7] Maurice Merleau-Ponty, *Sens et non-sens*, Paris, 1948, page 126.

[8] The development of historical consciousness, the awareness that we emerge from a history, is a temptation to understand the present exclusively from the past. We forget very easily that the past can offer explanations only after, and to the extent that it iself has become understandable through the present.

phenomenon. This is what actually happens when Marxism claims that the lower level of society determines the upper level. Rationality, the way of thinking, is developed by observing the way in which people work and utilize the world.

The error of Marxism consists in disregarding the unity of rationality and matter. This unity is evident when we consider the way in which a child appropriates the human world. He does so by materialized rationality, which is behavior. The child adopts patterns of behavior and, because he is intelligent, he is susceptible to its rationality and his intellect awakens. Nothing exemplifies this better than the phenomenon of the child's learning how to talk, for talking is certainly a form of behavior. The speaking of words is, as Merleau-Ponty says, a way in which we use the body. Speaking is the result of a contraction of the throat and a modulation of the vocal sound by the position of mouth and tongue.[9] The child imitates speech by producing meaningless sounds, and then he gradually discovers the meaning attached to certain words. This is the way in which he arrives at understanding. He does not understand before he learns how to talk, rather it is through speaking that he becomes familiar with the human world.

Merleau-Ponty. This naturally brings us to a consideration of Merleau-Ponty's explanation. According to his point of view, we become familiar with the world by discovering and analyzing the potentialities of what he calls the "ego-body." The world in which we live, thus he begins his analysis, is designed by and for man. It is adapted, adjusted to his fundamental possibilities. Whoever apprehends the meaning of a chair sees the structure of the human body. A car, a doorknob, a handbag, all utilities are made to conform to the grasping possibilities of the human hand. The size of a room in a house is determined basically by the size of the body. Language is created to conform with the speech possibilities of our speech organs. A world beyond the possibilities of man would no longer be a human world.

Merleau-Ponty's vision is valuable, but it does not suffice to explain the human realm of meaning. It is not possible to deduct the world of meaning from the potentialities of the "ego-body," because a possibility as a possibility is not knowable to us but is recognized only in its actualization. We know, in fact, more about the human possibilities than the cave-man, because we have *realized* them to a greater extent.

4. Human Encounter

A. We Become Familiar with Things Through Human Encounter

Intelligence, behavior, and the fundamental possibilities of the "ego-

---

9   Maurice Merleau-Ponty, *Phénoménologie de la perception,* page 226.

body," therefore, play an important part in the process of becoming familiar with the world, *but they are operative only within interhuman encounter*. The child can take over the behavior of adults, because he is able to understand them. He appropriates the rationality which is embodied in the human world, because he is responsive to other people. He develops the possibilities of the "ego-body" only within human encounter. Encounter with the other man is the fundamental sphere of our existence. Meaningful behavior is communicable only within an encounter, through being-together. We do not learn to live together because we learn to exist in the same world, but within and because of interhuman encounter we begin to live in the same world. The child is taken into the human sphere to the extent that he learns being-together. Within the encounter with man we become familiar with the world. If one were to raise a child in a cultured and meaningful environment without allowing him ever to meet other people (supposing that this were possible), the child would not appropriate the rationality and meaning of this environment. The meaning of the things we use becomes evident after we have observed the people who use them and thus learn to understand the meaning of their behavior. We understand the human world because we understand man, and not vice versa.

Recent psychological research has discovered another fact which confirms our point. Only the child who has been raised in an emotionally stable human environment and who has been given love and affection, matures as a well-balanced personality, knowing his way in the world. If children receive technically perfect care, but are not loved and caressed, that is, if they do not grow up within the interhuman play of love, they will always remain underdeveloped human beings. An example of a psychological test made in Italy shows this very clearly. A number of girls were convicted of crimes which carried jail sentences. The sentences were suspended, however, and a concentrated effort was made to re-educate these girls. For a number of them the effort failed completely; for others it succeeded at least moderately. Later an attempt was made to determine the reasons for this difference. First, the hypothesis that the incorrigible girls had a lower intelligence was tested. It proved false. Some of these girls were far more intelligent then the ones who were corrigible. After long research and the testing of many theories, it was finally discovered that those girls who were not responsive to re-education had never experienced love and friendship during the early years of their lives.

Since love is the height of interhuman contact, this psychological research proves the extent to which we really grow to full humanity and how we really begin to live in a human way through encounter with other people. We become familiar with things because of a previous familiarity with people. We become sensitive to the world because of our sensitivity to other people.

B. An Answer to Some Objections

All this may sound very improbable to some people. There exist for us, they will say, significant fields of meaning, which precede and are independent of the interhuman encounter. The field of vision for example, with its abundance of lines and colors, with its impressive landscapes, is something already given in the encounter of "ego-body" and nature, in which there is no need of an intermediate human person. The same seems to hold for the field of sound. When I take a walk on a beautiful morning in spring, I am overwhelmed by the deep and soft reflection of sunlight, by the fine green nuances of colors in the foliage, by the wonderful singing of the birds. When I enjoy the fresh air and the pleasant temperatures, I seem to be living in a realm of meaning which has no connection with other people. As a matter of fact, many people prefer to take a walk by themselves on such a beautiful morning. The same is apparently true with respect to food and odors. In other words, there seems to be a field of experience for me which is independent of any human encounter. It was in this area that empiricism found the primordial data of knowledge and explained its system without considering the influence of our contact with other people.

This viewpoint, however, is erroneous. Whoever thinks this way takes our extensive field of perception for granted and regards it as a pure datum without questioning how we acquired meaning in this field of perception. No distinction is made between the original meaningless field of perception and the one filled with significance. He should become acquainted with Marx' ideas about the poor perception of primitive man and the rich experience and perception of the man who, in a civilized society, has become human in a fuller sense. It is in and through interhuman encounter that the empty field of perception becomes meaningful. There is a distinction between undifferentiated, vague perception and true seeing. We learn to see, to listen, to taste in a fully human sense within being-together with our fellow men.

The meaning which empiricists denote as primordial is not as original as they claim. Again and again it is assumed that from a vague and undifferentiated horizon, meaningful elements gradually detach themselves. This, however, is not an automatic process, but is always connected with the human encounter, with being-together. If we would make a safari through the African jungle where very primitive natives live, our perceptional view is, at least materially, the same as theirs. Still we do not see the jungle as they do. The rich luxuriance of vegetation and the wild beauty of the scenery is probably not seen by the natives as such. And *we* do not see the things which are useful and significant to those primitive people. In the text of Merleau-Ponty, which we quoted above, he speaks of values, absolute valuations and meanings supposedly given with the "ego-body." This goes somewhat too far. Contact between "ego-body" and world does not produce explicit values and meanings. These values and meanings are mere possibilities in this realm, which become reality only through interhuman encounter.

C. Inner and Related Value of Human Encounter

This being-together-with-others takes place in the world, it makes the world familiar to us. But this interhuman encounter also has its own inner sense. We also seek it for its own sake. This becomes clear if we analyze the nature of a feast. A feast takes place in a little world of its own, usually a room festively arranged for the occasion. Drinks are served not just to quench thirst. The meal goes beyond the purpose of appeasing hunger. All kinds of dishes are put on the table which are a delight to behold and to savor. There is singing just for the sake of singing. Here, being-together does not serve an ulterior purpose, as in the case of labor, but everything serves the purpose of being-together, of interhuman relationships. Nothing is purely utilitarian. Guests do not talk to solve problems or to find truths. They talk, well, because talking in this atmosphere is just pleasant. Meaningful entertainment and relaxation are often sought and found in being-together. Being-together or human encounter, as we have seen in this chapter, is the origin of many meanings.

Apparently, however, it has an inner meaning in itself also which transcends other forms of meaning. St. Augustine once wrote in a letter: *"Nihil homini amicum sine homine amico."*[10] Freely translated, we could interpret these words as: All values lose their splendor outside human love. St. Augustine suggests further that we imagine the following: a man lives in a beautiful home in the most wonderful surroundings imaginable. He has everything he needs so far as food, drink, and relaxation are concerned, and he has an interesting and well-stacked library. However, if this person were to exist in this world all by himself, all these luxuries would be an unbearable hell for him. Poverty shared with others is preferable to the solitary enjoyment of riches, if one can speak of "enjoyment" here. Being-together is the most meaningful experience we know. Even truth and beauty would not continue to appeal to us outside of our being-together. Marxism thinks of being-together much too objectively and binds it too strongly to the infra-

---

[10] Augustine, *Epistolae,* 130, c. II, no. 4; P. L. 33, 495.

structure.[11] It does not regard sufficiently the specific and inner meaning of being-together. It reduces friendship too much to the comradeship of the world of labor.

Apart from being an independent value, being-together-with-others is also the fundamental realm in which all other values are disclosed. Even as colors and contours are brought out by a bright light, so are all values disclosed through being-together. Just as the painter likes to go to places where there is abundant light in order to see things better, so does man desire to experience values by this being-together-with-others. Being-together is not just the height of all values, and not just the realm in which all things receive their splendor; it is also the origin of our world of meaning.

We do not wish, however, to disregard the function of the intellect, or to minimize the importance of human labor stated by Marx. We do not deny the fundamental significance of the interchange between "ego-body" and world. But the fundamental form of knowledge comes to us through an understanding of one another, and it is within this mutual understanding that the world assumes meaning and significance for us. Working together is only one of the aspects of being-together. The dialectics of our body and world acquires its human level through the understanding of one another. This is truly a fundamental form of human existence.

It is also in close agreement with Christian doctrine, because it teaches that the ultimate fulfilment of our life is found in being-together with God, or rather in being-together-with-others in God. Our destiny has sometimes been described too one-sidedly as contemplation. This idea originated in a certain intellectualism, but is not in conformity with revelation.

---

11 Marxism is in its very essence a social philosophy. It teaches that man through experience and wants is limited to the world. However, this limitation is a task rather than a mere given fact. Man becomes himself by realizing his confinement to the world. This realization, according to Marxism, is conceivable only in social relationship. All that man is, in the realms of experience and the satisfaction of his wants, he is through human society and history. However, when Marx began to analyze this social self-realization, he awarded absolute primacy to the development of the means of production and arrived at the thesis that all other aspects of man's development are determined by it. We should keep in mind that Marx regarded the development of production as the development of human contact with the world, so that man was not determined by the non-human. Actually we may say that in Marx's estimation the whole of human existence was determined by one of its aspects. We should acknowledge, however, that in an era of individualism Marx sharply realized the fundamental significance of man's social being.

CHAPTER FOUR

BEING-TOGETHER AND "WORD"

1. *Intermingling of Thought and "Word"*

The social nature of the "word" has always been recognized insofar as language is defined as "a means of communication." This definition implies social contact. Sometimes, however, this communication aspect has been overemphasized, and as a result language may seem accidental to thought, a pure medium of communication.[1] This idea attributes to language little or no importance in the birth and origin of thought. It assumes that language presupposes completed thought and serves only as its outward manifestation.

This line of thinking is in perfect agreement with the individualistic philosophy of the near past. Man who, thanks to his long history, attained a highly developed personal existence within society, ignored the long and difficult way he had had to go. The main philosophical systems in this era of individualism adhered to this viewpoint.

Descartes indicated "clear and distinct ideas" as the innate origin of all intellectual light. It is not easy to ascertain the exact meaning of this Cartesian terminology, but this much is clear: the basic intellectual light does not depend upon language, society and history.

Empiricism pointed to the meaningful elements of perception as the basic components of our cognitive life, but these components were without relation to our social contact. Thus it is not surprising that the empiricist philosopher *Hobbes* regarded society as the product of a social contract. Man, he held, does not grow up and mature in and through society, but society itself is a human creation.

Late Scholasticism claimed to have found the source of all knowledge in the primordial experience of being and the self-evident principles of the intellect. It emphasized along the same lines that this primordial knowledge is a gift of nature and independent of our being-together. This idea was extended to the practical order by asserting that the law of nature was self-evident to the person, independently of our social life. The same line of thought is found everywhere: the human individual,

---

[1] In scholastic philosophy there is sometimes a tendency to underestimate the function of the word. The distinction between word and idea at times is presented as a separation. This is probably connected with the fact that, after scholastic thinking reached its height, it was undermined and attacked by nominalism, which attributed a very important function to the word. The tendency of scholasticism to minimize the function of the word grew as a reaction against nominalism. While reading this chapter, one should keep in mind that the author considers the word as the incarnation of thought, as permeated with the idea.

as distinct from society, is presented as the primary source of all explanations.

This individualism is slowly becoming a thing of the past. Contemporary philosophy no longer takes these so-called self-evident principles for granted, but tries to penetrate into the origin of our knowledge. In so doing, it has discovered the many ways in which the social is interwoven with the personal. This is also the case when we consider the nature of the "word." It is no longer possible to regard the "word" simply as a means of communication for a pre-existent thought. Thought and word appear to be intermingled. This is a first indication of the social nature proper to thought.

2. *The Explanation of Merleau-Ponty*

To our knowledge, it is Merleau-Ponty who most clearly expresses the contemporary awareness of the social character proper to thought. He gives three reasons which in our opinion prove the interpenetration of word and thought and, consequently, prove the social nature of thought. We do not mean that Merleau-Ponty is the originator of these new ideas, but he is the one who has most eminently interpreted and expressed this new awareness. True, we find valuable indications of it in Heidegger, but his thoughts in this matter are obscured by the fact that he places his philosophy of the "word" in the light of "being" and fails to state clearly what he means by "being."[2] It is for this reason that we prefer the clear and enlightening explanation of Merleau-Ponty.

The latter begins by observing that "thought seeks the word as its completion."[3] Introspection does not demonstrate at all that thought is first completed internally and that next we seek the proper word for it. We have rather the impression that thought, seeking its verbal expression, is seeking itself. Certainly, we cannot identify thought and its verbal expression. Everyone who really thinks knows that he sometimes sees a promising light, a perspective offering mental enlightenment. Such a perspective may open itself during profound reflective thinking in a study, during a conversation in which one really communicates with another, or during a lecture or speech. As a matter of fact, the idea which is elaborated in this book was born while the author was giving a lecture. In such a situation, suddenly a horizon of light appears. There is a vision which precedes speaking, and from it speaking and writing originate.

---

[2] The philosophy of Heidegger has a strongly social character. In *Sein und Zeit* he describes our existence as being-with-others (pages 114-130). It is strange, however, that he discovers the presence of "the others" in things and proceeds from things to man. In *Grundformen und Erkenntniss menschlichen Daseins* L. Binswanger claims that Heidegger's approach is onesided, because the latter does not pay sufficient attention to the unique nature of being-together in love. Binswanger's book contains an abundance of data and some very rich analyses, but it lacks synthesis.

[3] *Phénoménologie de la perception,* page 206.

Merleau-Ponty does not evaluate this phenomenon sufficiently, since he calls it a "silence" which seeks expression.[4] But it is more than silence, it is a vision. Those who are familiar with reflective thinking know that such a perspective or vision is not necessarily a valuable one. It may happen that we experience a perspective as extremely valuable but an effort to express it and put it into words proves to be rather unfruitful. On the other hand, it also may happen that what seems a rather unfruitful perspective turns out to be very valuable once it has been expressed in words. This proves that a vision is not completed before its expression. It seeks its expression and demonstrates its value only after its verbal form is completed. A new vision is more a promise than a completed reality. A thought, an idea reaches its fulfilment when it is embodied in words. For this reason little value can be attached to the often-heard excuse of a student who is being examined: "I know the answer, Sir, but I am unable to put it into words." True, we may realize that our words inadequately express what we mean and be uneasily aware of the fact that our expressions fail to do full justice to our thought. Nevertheless, it remains true that where there is genuine understanding, there is also a possibility of expression, no matter how inadequate our words may be.

The idea that thought becomes itself in speech is concordant with the deeper essence of man. Man is embodied consciousness. The body is not a kind of living quarters for a spirit living a life all of its own. The spirit exists, realizes itself in the body. This has already been pointed out in a previous chapter. Just as the person comes into full existence through embodiment, so does the thought, the idea exist in the word.

Therefore, says Merleau-Ponty, "the naming of objects does not follow their recognition, but *is* this recognition itself."[5] This second reason is an extension of the first. As long as we are seeking the name of someone or something, we are seeking the reality itself. The "word" does not point to a reality which already existed for us before it was named, but on the contrary it makes this reality exist for us. The "word" is not an accidental indication of a pre-existing vision, but it makes this vision exist.

In the book of Genesis, it is written that Adam called all things by their names. This means that Adam knew these things, that he made them exist for himself and brought them to light. Te speak, to name is

---

[4] *Phénoménologie de la perception,* pages 462-463. This is one of the weakest points of Merleau-Ponty's philosophy. It is here that he is unfaithful to experience. St. Augustine, on the contrary, often expressed this experience in a masterful way. The former rhetorician always kept a great respect for the word. In his analyses he frequently speaks about the birth of the word from an enlightening perspective. St. Augustine recognizes that this perspective of light requires the word, but he also knows that at times the latent richness of vision transcends verbal expression. He knew from experience that certain visions remain "ineffable." Merleau-Ponty underestimates the value of this experience.

[5] *Phénoménologie de la perception,* page 207.

to bring to light. As long as a thing is unnamed by man, it is submerged in a realm of obscurity. Through being named it emerges as a point of light in the world. To name a thing is to grasp it, to master it. In his speaking, man manifests himself as the king of the universe. Thus the respect for names in the Old Testament was fully justified. During the past long period of individualism, we have lost this respect, because we were blind to the profound significance of man's ability to speak and to name.

Finally there is a third, very convincing reason.[6] We become familiar with an unknown thought or idea through the "word." When we read the works of a philosopher whose ideas are not known to us, we gradually become familiar with his thought, and this happens only by way of the "word." We would not become acquainted with his thinking if it were not embodied in words.

One could try to weaken the convincing force of this argument by saying that a particular philosopher uses words in a new association. The elements are therefore known to us, but the association is new. If this were true the argumentation would be indeed inconclusive. One would then continue to distinguish the meaning of things in the intellect from that in their verbal expression. New combinations of words would make us familiar with new combinations of thought, the latter being distinct from the word-combinations.

This objection, however, is not valid for the simple reason that wherever there are truly new ideas, the words expressing them also acquire new meaning. We can experience this when, leaving the positivistic, Kantian or scholastic worlds of thought, we begin to read the works of Heidegger or Merleau-Ponty. All kinds of familiar words are encountered, but we do not notice initially that these words and expressions do not have the familiar meaning. Consequently, we read and interpret most of them wrongly. Gradually, however, we notice the new way of speaking and the new meaning of words. Only after this discovery is it possible to enter into the new thought. Indeed we have *new* thought here and not just new combinations of old elements. For this reason, one understands a philosophical book only after reading the last chapter and then the deeper meaning of the first chapter becomes clear. A new philosophy breathes a new spirit with which one becomes familiar only gradually. How do we become acquainted with this new way of thinking? There is only one medium: "the word." Therefore, we must conclude that thought is really present in words. To learn someone's language is identical with penetrating into his thought.

3. The "Word," as the Origin of Truth and Evidence

If thought exists in "word" and if "word" or language is a social

---

[6]   *Op. cit.*, pages 208-209.

phenomenon, it follows that thought is essentially social too. Once we have accepted that thinking and speaking are interwoven and are situated in the social realm, we may approach this matter from two viewpoints.

First, we may point out, as Merleau-Ponty does over and over again, that all intellectual light rests on a foundation of darkness. The understanding of verbal expressions may give us an illusion of insight and enlightenment. When we listen to the lecture of a genial philosopher, and when we follow his words with understanding, we seem to live in a world of light and vision. We actually live then in the speaker's world of light and enter into his vision. But closer reflection reveals that this light is rooted in darkness. Merleau-Ponty points out that even the most illuminating insights contain factors which are not brought to light.[7] There are self-evidences which are no longer self-evident after more profound reflection. It is apparently perfectly evident to us, for example, that two plus two equals four. We may however, ask the question, what is the meaning of "two," "four," "plus" and "equals"? This so-called evidence submerges again into darkness, as is known too well by those who occupy themselves with the philosophy of mathematics.

Merleau-Ponty comes, therefore, to the following conclusion: all evidence is essentially ambiguous. The evidence exists only as long as we put ourselves within a definite horizon, within a generally accepted terminology, and do not question this horizon or terminology itself. No absolute evidence is possible. We are receptive to the extent of the actual light given us. If we, therefore, stop seeking perfect and complete evidence—an illusion of exaggerated rationalism—we may experience an insight of limited evidence.

One may also approach this matter from another viewpoint. Speaking, putting thoughts into words, is animated thinking. Speaking, therefore, is the birth of light, the bringing to light. For this reason it is possible that speaking is the embodiment of insight, real insight which fully convinces, in such a manner that we say "yes," without fearing the possibility of a "no." True, this light leads a frail existence, but it *is* light. This light, this evidence, this vision is born within a contingent horizon, because no valuable form of evidential light can exist unless human speech and language have reached a certain level of maturity. The evidence of truth exists for us, although we do not know how it came to be.

We may compare this situation to the understanding of a work of art. Whoever sees and appreciates the paintings of Rembrandt or listens with understanding to the music of Bach, lives in a world of light. He probably does not understand at all where this light comes from, how it originates in him, but it is not necessary to know this in order to live in this world of light and vision. The same is true also of the word.

---

[7]   *Op. cit.*, pages 450-455.

We do not know how convincing evidence can come into existence within the fragile reality of words, but nevertheless it does exist and compels us to an affirmation. We do not understand how the interaction between the eye and the world around us produces the rich, bright field of vision, but we do see and experience it. Deeper reflection on the existence of light for the eye and light for the mind reveals a great miracle and a great mystery, but it does not take away the fact that they do exist and affect us.

We accept, therefore, with Merleau-Ponty that the "word" which is permeated with thinking, is the origin of truth, evidence and light, but we hold fast also to the fact that truth, evidence and light really and truly exist. It is not right to deny evidence because we do not understand how we arrived at it. Merleau-Ponty confuses two problems—namely, the problem of existence of this evidential light and that of its ultimate possibility. Because it is impossible for him to explain the ultimate possibility of truth, he denies its existence. In spite of all his protest against rationalism, he himself falls here into the rationalistic pit.

But is it not the task of the philosopher, one may ask, to search for the ultimate foundations? Should he not reject this so-called evidence as an illusion, so long as he has not found its ultimate foundations? This objection merely seems to be a strong argument. Our answer is that evidence *itself* carries convincing force and is therefore itself the foundation of its strength. This light of evidence does not owe its force to the way in which it came to be. In the verbal expression itself a vision lives, or rather, comes into being, even though we do not understand how this is possible. We must accept our experience. In judging experience, Merleau-Ponty is prejudiced by a theory.

4. The "Word" as Developed in Language is a Social Phenomenon

Our thinking, as interwoven with verbal expression, is by its very nature social. We attain to thinking because we are born into a speaking society. Naturally we do have a power of thinking, but this potency comes to a state of realization only because it is aroused and called forth by society. We live in a society in which thinking, through a long history, has come to light. This light exists in verbal expression, be it in speech or in writing. For this reason we are able to appropriate intellectually in a few years what it has taken mankind centuries to discover. This is a great privilege: we enter into the speech and language of our time and, as a result, enter into its light also. In order to accomplish this, it is necessary that we make this language fully our own. Instead of becoming parrotlike repeaters, we should begin to live truly in this light which is embodied in speech.

Now it becomes understandable that children of different nationalities learn to think in different ways. The average Frenchman thinks differently from the average German. They speak, they express their thoughts differently. This means that a different way of thinking is present in every language. People enter into these different ways of thinking through language; consequently wherever the same language is spoken there prevails a general similarity of thinking. Americans think like Americans. Sometimes they may learn a foreign language thoroughly and even enter into the thinking of another nation, but they still remain Americans who understand the thinking of other peoples.

It follows that we should have a great respect for our language. We owe our way of thinking to it. The thinking of a nation lives embodied in its language. Thanks to language, we take part in a precious heritage. We are most ungrateful if we do not use our language with respect. Lack of respect for the language is really rooted in a lack of self-respect. It is, therefore, alarming that many young people have little or no respect for their mother tongue.

What is the significance of the social nature of language, the embodiment of thought? We might describe the present languages as fixed, established modes of human encounter. Because of the social nature of language, to speak does not mean merely a way in which we give expression to a thought in so many words, but it is as Merleau-Ponty holds, also essentially a way of human encounter, human involvement. It would be wrong to think of language as a tool of encounter which is readily available and of which anyone may avail himself at will, with little or no personal involvement. Certainly, language has *also* the aspect of being an objective datum. In grammars and dictionaries language is treated from a purely objective viewpoint, which might lead us to believe that language is divorced from all personal human involvement. But the analysis of the preceding pages has pointed clearly to a subjective aspect of language. We have shown that language is embodied thought. Thought itself is actualized in language. We may say that thought flows through language as through a channel.[8]

We do not mean that thought is definitely crystallized in language, because thought is always creative and may therefore transform a language in a creative new way. This accounts for the continuous changes in a living language. Thought may allow itself to be channelled, but it cannot be confined. However, when thought is creatively being developed, it must start from the actual language in which it came into being. Thought is, therefore, indeed channelled in language, and this channelling even affects its movement toward the future.

---

[8] It is obvious, therefore, that the structures of thinking are present in language. The philosophical and linguistic analyses of the judgment use the same terms. The temporal structure of our thinking is reflected in the different tenses of the verb. Forms of thinking are revealed in the words which denote connection between sentences as, for instance, and, but, because, although, and if.

5. *Language is a Human Encounter*

Because people belong to the same society of language, they live in the same world of thought. Language is therefore an encounter which has taken form in the world. This is also true for the entire manipulatable world of which we spoke in the preceding chapters. Each man-made instrument requires a certain way of manipulative behavior. If we use the world together, there must be a common behavior in this use. Thus a common language is conceivable only if there is a common way of thinking.

This community of thought is not contradicted by the fact that people who speak the same language often disagree and argue. This fact rather affirms the point we are making, because a discussion is possible only between people who communicate in the same world of thought. If a discussion is no longer possible, we live in different worlds and as a consequence develop different languages. Thus, up to recently, a discussion between a Marxist politician and a Catholic theologian was inconceivable. They did not speak the same language. There was a time in which Catholic and Protestant theologians could barely speak with one another. Because for centuries they had travelled along diverging paths, they had lost contact with each other, which in turn manifested itself in a profound difference of theological speech. If the language of many people is really the same, they must live in a common world of thought.

Language indicates two things. First, it points to the things spoken of, which have become manifest through language. Secondly, it indicates the people who together use that language. This second point is not at all accidental. The language which I use is not my invention. I have learned to bring things to light in this special fashion, because I belong to this special society of speech.

These two indications are present in the same language; it is not possible that they could have a separate existence. Every language is a bringing-to-light, a making manifest of the world in community with other people. Again, thinking appears here as a social phenomenon.[9] Even when I go into solitude in order to think creatively, my thinking is on the social level. I can do this only because I am part of a society which, through language is making the world intelligible. When I am thinking, I am therefore continuing a common undertaking. I am situated within a social endeavor. Because I have obligations to my

---

[9] "The *object-for-us* finds its origin in the word." Stephan Strasser, "Het wezen van de mens," *De mens, inleidingen voor de algemene vergadering te Leuven en Brussel van het wijsgerig gezelschap en de vereniging voor thomistische wijsbegeerte,* Utrecht, 1958, page 16. (Reprinted from *De Annalen van het Thijmgenootschap*). This lecture recognizes the social dimension of our existence. Although this dimension is not the theme of the lecture, it permeates Strasser's thinking as a general background.

language society, this society in its turn has a right to the benefit of my thinking. I have discovered the world through my social existence; new discoveries made by me in the realm of the intellect belong, therefore, to the society in which I have been reared.

6. *The Sciences are Modes of Human Encounter*

All this is of great importance in the philosophy of science. Science may be described from this perspective. The different sciences, it is said, are distinguished from one another by their difference of object. A different object means a different science. A purely material difference of object, of course, is not a criterion for distinguishing different sciences. A cat and a dog are different, but they are still objects of the same science. There must be a formal distinction of object, that is, not of the object as an exterior thing, but precisely of the object as object of science. Therefore different things may belong to the realm of the same science and one thing may be the object of many sciences. Animal psychology considers many kinds of animals but, on the other hand, man can be the object of several sciences, such as medical, psychological, and theological sciences.

The object considered scientifically causes a distinction between sciences in as many ways as it is regarded by man as an object. Being-object means therefore being, "ob-jected", placed before man. The object as object is determined by the subject who is considering it. There is, consequently, a distinction between sciences because, and to the extent in which, man in his thinking approaches things in different ways. However, we do not want to reduce everything to man, for the way of approach should also fit the object. We shall never have clarity in the problem of the distinction between sciences if we fix our attention exclusively either on thinking man or on the object. We can understand the distinction between the sciences only if we consider object and subject simultaneously in their interaction.

The history of the sciences is therefore a history of approaches.[10] This history includes man in his quest of knowledge as well as the object. It comprises both the knower as the one who brings to light and the object as the thing which is brought to light. The way of approach is not arbitrary nor is it a ready-to-apply datum. It is not the result of free imagination, but neither do we find it "already" established in the things to be approched.

---

[10] Scholastic philosophy has always viewed the distinction and the division of the sciences neither from an absolute object-pole nor from an absolute subject-pole, but from the correlationship of the two. Some scholastic philosophers, however, hoped to find absolute aspects in this correlation, from which an absolute and everlasting division of the sciences might be constructed. Undoubtedly, there are necessary and absolute aspects in the subject-object relation, but these aspects may be taken in many ways in the development of thinking. The distinction and division of the sciences are therefore subject to the historical evolution of thought to a greater extent than had been hitherto suspected.

Where does the approach find its foundation? Here we must again regard the two poles: subject and object. Because of his nature, man is destined to approach the world in a human way. The fact that we are "open" to the world through eyes and ears, hands and feet is not at all accidental. These senses are fundamental possibilities of approach. On the other hand, the things themselves are not approachable in just any way either in the realm of knowledge or in the practical field. Man always finds himself in a definite situation, but this situation leaves him free to a certain extent, since there are still many possibilities. On the one hand, he must determine his way of approach but, on the other, he is bound by certain standards. Man in this respect is neither entirely free nor entirely bound. He finds himself on a road on which he may continue in various directions. This mixture of freedom and restriction does not exist only at the beginning of the road, but it is always present.

At the beginning of the different ways of approach—which are the beginnings of science—language plays a decisive role. Thought "exists" in language, as we have said before. The scientific way of approach also exists in language. The expression "exists in" must be understood in the samy way as existentialist philosophy understands its expression "man exists in the body." No identification is intended here. In order to avoid ambiguity, it might be better therefore to say that the way of approach comes into existence in language. It is there that the way of approach becomes manifest, takes shape, and becomes what it is. Language is by nature a social phenomenon. Thus the birth of the scientific approach is a social fact, it is the development of a social encounter with the world. The sciences therefore come into existence as a result of the ways in which man encounters the world.

Is not, we may ask, the term "encounter" here used in a metaphorical sense? For the proper sense of "encounter" is used only in connection with meetings between people. There are two reasons why this objection is not entirely true.[11]

In the first place, science as knowledge of an object, is always a real encounter with people. It is science which makes the world manifest in language, and human language is essentially intersubjective. The study of science therefore means taking part in a joint dialogue. In order to study science, one must enter into this dialogue which is already in progress. Today this is achieved through education. It is not sufficient materially to know current scientific terminology, but one must also attain understanding and become familiar with the content of the terms. It is true that thereafter a person may continue alone, but even then, one carries onward the development of a joint dialogue. The study of science is thus conceivable only as an encounter between people.

---

11   The use of the term "encounter" with respect to the infra-human world may seem to be metaphorical. However, when we see that our encounter with nature lies contained within the encounter with man we will realize that the use of this term is unequivocal and proper.

Certainly, it is a channelled encounter, but still it is a real human encounter.

Secondly, we should realize, as has been demonstrated above, that it is our fellow men who are accessible to us first and foremost. We become familiar with the non-human world through our communication with them. This is very obvious in the sphere of the sciences. They make us familiar with objects, but only through the medium of language, and language is a human phenomenon. We are sensitive to the light existing in language, because we have an openness towards our fellow men. We become familiar with the field of scientific thinking because, and to the extent that we are familiar with human existence. It is not true that we become familiar with a certain science, and subsequently enter into a new kind of contact with our fellow men. No, the field of science is accessible to us *because* we are familiar with man and with whatever is characteristic of man. The encounter with the object of the sciences is possible because we are able to encounter man.

Thus, if we use the term "encounter" for the study of sciences, we are not guilty of using metaphorical language. This assertion is fully in harmony with the fundamental idea of this book—namely, that we are basically and primarily familiar with man, and through him with the rest of the world. Our fundamental thesis receives a new confirmation. The familiarity of the scientist with his field of thinking appears to be a form of our familiarity with man. We may describe the different sciences as ways of human encounter which have been developed through the course of centuries. It is here that we find the key of a new approach to the explanation of the distinctions between the many sciences. At this point, it will be necessary, therefore, to analyze language more profoundly as a social encounter.

7. *The Scientific Approach as Encounter. A Further Analysis*

Language is man's grasp of things. It is not a physical grasping as with the hands. When we grasp things with our hands, whether directly or indirectly through tools, we effect a change in the world. This is a real physical change which continues to exist also after we have taken our hands off the things. The "word" and its development in language is a more refined grasp, which leaves things untouched in their physical reality, but affects them in their meaning for us. Through speech things become meaningful; they manifest themselves to our intellect.[12] Just as physical grasping is adapted to the grasping powers of our body as well

---

[12] "You should not be surprised that the discussion of the essence of nihilism unavoidably encounters at every point in the road something worthy of stimulating thinking, which we awkwardly enough call the language of thinking. This language is not the expression of thinking, but is thinking itself, its stride and its voice." Martin Heidegger, *The Question of Being*, Twayne Publishers, New York, 1958, p. 105. Translation of William Kluback and Jean T. Wilde.

as to the nature of things, so also should the apprehending "word" be adapted to the two poles which govern this grasping.[13]

Further reflection upon our physical grasping of things—significantly this is also called *"handling"*—shows that there are differences in the ways in which we grasp lifeless matter, plants, animals, and man. Lifeless matter behaves rather passively whenever we handle it. The handling of plants requires a certain care, for we have to respect the laws governing their lives and the environment they need. The approach to an animal requires more understanding and know-how. An animal is temperamental and may feel ill or well at ease. The wrong approach to a horse, for instance, may irritate or frighten it, so that it will try to kick us. Contact with man is again an entirely different matter. He is a free being; and only after he has made himself available to us freely, are we able to get in touch with him. Let us recall that we are more familiar with man and that within the interhuman encounter we learn to "handle" other realities appropriately. At first this may seem improbable, because lifeless matter can so easily be handled by man. However, we should not be deceived by appearances; it is within the sphere of contact with people that we learn to manage the infrahuman.

The grasping power of the "word" likewise varies according to the realm which we approach. If the realities to be put into words have a less proper and less independent existence, the grasping power will be greater. The grasping potencies of language are greatest in the realm of mathematics, where the intellect is all-powerful. The "wording" thought can operate in this realm according to its own dynamics; the object does not resist; as an "almost nothing," it has no actuality in virtue of which it could resist. It is here that man is able to designate precisely and univocally what he wants to put into words: the object does not withdraw from the designating power of the word. Inorganic matter, the object of physics and chemistry, may also be expressed in a univocal and exact way by means of the word. As it is grasped passively in the physical order, it is also expressed in words effortlessly and exactly.

However, as soon as we try to name what is alive, precisely as living, the designating power of the "word" seems to weaken. Just as the farmer must be more careful with his crop than with the soil, so must the scientist be more careful in applying the "word" to living objects than to inorganic matter. Living things, such as plants, have within themselves the power to change form, to take on a new appearance; they are essentially dynamic. It is true that one might formulate laws about them, but the content of the law is more difficult to describe, and its

---

[13] "A meaning may emerge if things are *actively* gathered and arranged in orderly fashion. To establish a meaning is always the result of a transformation of things through labor, which then transcends itself in the verbal expression of the things. Labor and language are the two original and inseparable roots of all culture." A. de Waelhens, "De mens en cultuur," *De Mens* (see footnote 9), page 64.

absolute validity, if we may use this word, is more difficult to prove. An attempt to describe the animal world by means of words is even more difficult, as is obvious from the scientific discussions on this subject. What, for example, is the meaning of the word "seeing," when we apply it to an animal? There are phenomena which lead us to believe that an animal, a horse for example, "sees," but the precise meaning of this "seeing" escapes us. To describe the human realm in words is the most difficult of all. Anyone who has ever tried to put into words human realities, such as knowledge, love, and friendship, knows this very well. In brief, just as there is a progressive difficulty in "handling" things which have a higher form of existence, so does the grasping power of the "word" become more ambiguous as the things described are of a higher order.

It would seem that we are now undermining our own thesis. This book is supposed to be written to demonstrate that man is more familiar to us in terms of knowledge than are things, and we even claim that it is through man that we learn to know the other things. But the preceding paragraphs seem to show that the objects of mathematics and of the natural sciences are more familiar to us. It is in these areas that the grasping power of the human word is the greatest. Here, therefore, lies the ground and reason for the scientistic attitude, which wants to approach all things with the intellectual methods of the exact sciences. This is the foundation of the fact, indicated in the first chapter, that certain psychologies approach and understand man in the same fashion as physical science follows with regard to nature. Is it true, then, that nature is better manageable and better known than is man?

Superficially it may seem so, but this is only appearance. The exact language which reveals to me the objects of nature and of mathematics, is itself a human phenomenon, and I understand it because I am familiar with human phenomena. The object of mathematics exists and is accessible for me precisely because, and to the extent that, it is expressed in the human phenomenon of language. A prerequisite for the understanding of an object is an understanding of the language and, consequently, an understanding of the human realm. The openness toward the other man remains primary, and within this openness for the other I have access also to non-human objects.

This is a general refutation of the objection raised. We feel, however, that a further disproof of this objection is necessary because apparent truth is so much in its favor.

Above we have described the sciences as ways of encounter which find expression in language. They are a collective dialogue between man and reality. We are a part of this dialogue, because we have an openness toward man. If a science is more specialized, however, the way of encounter will be more channelled, more purified of elements which do not belong in that particular way of encounter. Specialized science is a purified dialogue, drained of foreign elements, held in univocal terms, raised to a high degree of lucidity. This is the reason why mathematics has such a great attraction for the human intellect. Here is a lucidity which is not found elsewhere. This is to a great extent also true of the natural sciences.

It would, however, be a serious mistake to conclude that we are more familiar with *the objects* of mathematics and of the natural sciences than with man. As we have mentioned, familiarity with these objects depends upon our familiarity with man. The facts are in agreement with this statement. As long as we move about in the sphere of mathematics we are in the clarity of a purified dialogue. But as soon as we ask the question—and with this question we step out of the dialogue itself— what exactly do we know in this science, the answer seems to be rather difficult. The philosophy of mathematics still struggles with the reply in this highly rational dialogue. The same is true of the natural sciences. As long as we remain in the realm of the natural sciences, we are living in a world of clarity—even though it is difficult to enter into this world because of the highly refined nature of this dialogue. But as soon as we ask a scientist *what* he really *knows* in his particular science and what the reality indicated by the word "nature" is, he finds himself in darkness.[14] The world of mere things, of the non-conscious, is a world of darkness for us, with which we can never identify ourselves.

It is also well known that, in spite of the great progress of science, we actually know very little about the intimate nature of vegetative life. We are slightly more familiar with the animal world, but much of it is still obscure, and we certainly cannot call it a world of clarity. But as soon as we enter the human realm, we live in a familiar world. We understand man directly and intuitively. We can share in his thinking and his feeling, we partake of his life. True, there will always remain depths of human existence which escape us, but that does not erase the fact that we have a real and direct understanding of man, which we do not have of any non-human objects.

We should therefore make a distinction between the pure, univocal, clear, and rational nature of a particular science, and this science as real understanding of, and familiarity with its object. It may sound paradoxical, but the two aspects are inversely proportionate. The more we are able to speak in a univocal and strictly rational fashion about a certain datum, the less it is familiar to us as a reality; and the more we are familiar with a reality, the more difficult it is to have a rational and univocal dialogue about it.

This paradox may seem strange at first. However, it is not beyond explanation. We have to keep in mind that the level of a reality is

---

14 In discussions with scientists we have often noticed that they found themselves in an impasse, whenever they were asked what exactly is known in their sciences. As long as scientists remain in their own science and can speak their own mathematical language they are in a world of light. As soon, however, as they want to express this "light" in "ordinary words" it turns into darkness.

proportioned to the level of its being, of its independent *existence*. The scientific "word," on the other hand, has the character of a grasp. The more independent a being is, the more this grasp will have to respect its proper character.

In such a case our grasping power will no longer depend only on the exactitude and the rationality of the word. The inner refinement of this grasping instrument will guarantee less and less the effectiveness of the grasp. When the object considered has a higher level of independence, the initiative of man's grasp renders success less and less secure, but man's openness for what is proper in the reality which he studies plays an ever increasing role. For this reason success is guaranteed in mathematics because of the utter refinement of the rational instrument. However, where the human being is concerned, one must make oneself receptive to the man who gives himself freely to us. The other must be given an opportunity to speak to us and we must be willing to be spoken to. The univocity of the grasping word is shattered by the richness of the reality to be grasped.

8. Summary

At the end of this chapter we would like to summarize the conclusions. Every science has the quality of a collective dialogue and is therefore by nature a social phenomenon. Because of our openness toward the other and our possibility to take part in a dialogue, we are able to render the world intelligible.

The problem of the distinction between the different sciences gains clarity when we approach it from its dialogue-like character. As long as we find ourselves in the same line of approach, the same sphere of dialogue, there are no essential distinctions among the sciences. For Aristotle, the natural sciences and philosophy were not distinct, because Aristotle knew only the philosophical approach. Modern man started a new dialogue with nature, and thereby new sciences were born.

The more exact a science is, the greater the clarity and lucidity of the collective dialogue. However, this does not mean that we become more familiar also with the object as a reality. On the contrary, it is man who has a primary familiarity for us. It is through our familiarity with man that we are able to enter into a dialogue, and through the dialogue we become familiar with all reality. Our fellow man is directly and primarily accessible to us and is a *conditio sine qua non* of our access to all other beings.

Those who think that the exactitude of mathematics is the ideal approach for all sciences commit a gross error. This approach is possible where the object offers little resistance and appears less as a partner in a dialogue. The more, however, the object is independent and the greater its own autonomy, the more must we be open to the object and the more must we acknowledge the weakening grasping power of the "word." Those who attempt to know man in the same fashion in which they know nature necessarily misunderstand and undervalue man. The equivocity and ambiguity of the "word" originate in the richness of reality.

These ideas are fundamental for a new evaluation of the sciences. To develop them will require a more precise indication of the different ways of encounter.

CHAPTER FIVE

METAPHYSICAL PERSPECTIVES

1. *The Possibility of Metaphysics*

When Andronicus of Rhodes, the catalogist of Aristotle's writings, called a number of books *"ta meta ta physica,"* i.e., the writings after the books about physics, he probably had no idea that he used a term which would become highly controversial in the history of philosophical thinking. Since then the term "metaphysics" has been taken to mean the effort or the human mind to arrive at meaningful assertions about "being as such," about the whole of reality. This effort may seem to be highly arrogant but, on the other hand, it is difficult to escape it.

Metaphysics seems to be an arrogant activity for man. Is he not an extremely limited and small being in the immense totality of time and space? We have access to reality by way of a few senses which, despite their importance, are limited in their capacity of introducing us to reality. We develop our cognitive life only through our participation in the history of a definite nation; contemporary Americans, for instance, cannot approach reality in any other way than as Americans of the twentieth century. It seems rather foolhardy to make assertions about the whole of reality from such a limited situation. For this and other reasons metaphysics seems to be a highly disputable activity, a contradictory phenomenon. Hence it is no small wonder that in almost every period of history we meet philosophers who deny the possibility of metaphysics. They base their negation on the fact that man's cognition is limited, that it is determined by time and space, that it is subject to an historical situation, confined to a certain society.[1]

Nevertheless it remains a striking fact that man is driven by an irresistible force to make meaningful assertions about the totality of being. For this reason it has been said that man suffers from "a metaphysical disease." We might even say that he had been suffering from this metaphysical disease even before he arrived at philosophical thinking in the strict sense of the term. Folk tales and myths precede philosophical thinking; and in them we find a desire to view all of reality. The Egyptian and Babylonian cosmogonies are stories about the origin and structure of reality. Although they are far from being couched in scientific terms, they do present an outlook upon being. The great metaphysician Plato often resorts to myths in his dialogues, and these passages frequently belong to the best of his writings. Plato's myths have a mysterious influence, which does not fail to impress even us, who are products of western rational thinking.

---

[1] Cf. John A. Peters, *Metaphysics,* Ch. VI nos 22-27 (to be published in *Duquesne Studies, Philosophical Series*).

Metaphysicians are of the opinion that the metaphysical "arrogance" in question is implicitly present in the systems of the more "modest" philosophers, who explicitly deny the possibility of metaphysics. Systems of thought which reject metaphysics may thus possess a hidden, metaphysical undercurrent. A classic example is positivism, which withdraws modestly into the realm of phenomena and rejects as absurd every effort to transcend the world of observable phenomena. A closer look, however, reveals that the realm of phenomena is seen as the whole of reality, and therefore we must classify positivism as a metaphysics of the *positum,* of the phenomenon. For the same reason contemporary materialistic philosophies are not to be classified as non-metaphysical; on the contrary they are materialistic metaphysics. The radical theory of evolution, for example, which is rapidly gaining ground, attempts to understand all forms of being, man included, from the basic principle of evolution, which is supposed to be the explanation of all being. The physical sciences of the present search for the ultimate formula of the universe; some scientists consider this a search for the ultimate and fundamental structure of the whole of reality. In this case the physical sciences are presented as a metaphysics.

The materialistic thinker Karl Marx speaks rather cynically of metaphysics,[2] but he himself vigorously indulges in metaphysical considerations. His thinking offers not only an outlook on being, but also a comprehensive view of it. However materialistic Marxism may be, it is a metaphysical system. In short, metaphysics may be rejected in words, but not in fact.

It is not our intention here to deal thoroughly with the problem of the possibility of metaphysics. In this chapter we merely wish to trace the metaphysical consequences of our initial thesis. The preceding considerations seem to be a fitting introduction. They make us aware of the fact that the way in which one approaches "being" is decisive for all of metaphysics. The so-called "modest" philosophers, followers of either subjectivism or relativism, draw our attention to the fact that we cannot view the *totality* of being from an imaginary point outside the total reality, but at most are able to have a view of reality from a limited situation. We must, therefore, accept that our situation is a limited viewpoint and that, reversely, the various possible views are determined in the situation.[3]

For this reason we may assert that the ultimate metaphysical viewpoint of a philosopher is already implied in his description of our cognitive situation. One who considers the physical sciences as knowledge *par excellence,* as the only possible knowledge, declares at the same time that man is blind to everything outside this cognitive realm.

We have defended the thesis that our cognitive situation is dominated

---

[2]   Karl Marx, *Das Elend der Philosophie,* Dietz Verlag, Berlin 1957, p. 124.
[3]   Cf. Albert Dondeyne, *Contemporary European Thought and Christian Faith,* Pittsburgh, 1958, pages 27-28.

by a primary familiarity with the other person and that it is through this familiarity that we become acquainted with the rest of reality. We now must determine the metaphysical implications of this viewpoint.

2. *Metaphysics and Encounter*

Our viewpoint, as explained in the preceding chapters, may draw the suspicion of relativism. We say that through interhuman contact the world becomes familiar to us, that by naming things we transform them into a named world, and by cultivating and manipulating them we convert the world into an area under human control. Does this not mean that we are enclosed in a historically limited, human world? The entire realm of existence seems to be human. The transformation of the world into an area under human control means that everything in this world, at least potentially, is within the human grasp. Likewise, when we bring things to light by means of the human word, we seize them in a rather subtle, but still human grasp. Within the same historical human realm also man encounters his fellow man. We do not meet each other as naked, worldless persons, but precisely as human "existences." We come into being within this human world and we encounter one another within this human world.

Man, world, and the human encounter all occur in the same history. But, as such, are not man, world and encounter bound and limited by this history? There are indeed modern philosophers who think so. Merleau-Ponty, for example, describes history as the cradle of all meaning and as the location of each meaningful encounter. A particular type of unorthodox Marxism thinks along the same lines. It is found mainly in the early writings of G. Lucacs, who disengaged himself from Marxist determinism in order to put strong emphasis on the dialectics between man and world as the origin of all meaning. Later, he returned to Marxist orthodoxy, but his writings made a profound impression and proved a source of inspiration to a number of French philosophers.

We definitely do not wish to give the impression that we are followers of this line of thought. Our thesis does not lead to a closed perspective but to an *open* one. Man's restless spirit does not find its resting place in the world of encounter, but rather a new starting point.

The term "encounter" has two meanings which are distinct from but related to each other. "Encounter" means, first, intersubjective human relationships and, second, our relationships to the infra-human. We have thoroughly explained the distinction as well as the relationship between the two. We indicated the distinction by pointing to the familiarity which we have with other men while the infra-human remains obscure in a haze of strangeness. The relationship, on the other hand, was stressed by indicating that it is within the human encounter that the rest of the world becomes accessible to us.[4] History may indeed be described as the unfolding of the encounter. Within the encounter people find one another and through it they make the world a familiar living place. This perspective may be called the end of a study and considered to be its conclusion. At the same time, however, it is also a point of departure, for it raises a number of very fundamental problems, which lead us to new viewpoints and even to a new metaphysics. Let us develop these problems.

A. The Encounter with the Non-Human World

First of all, let us consider our relation to the infra-human world. We may say that we become familiar with this world by humanizing it. Immediately the question arises, how is it possible that the non-human world lets itself be humanized?

Modern currents of philosophy touch upon this problem when they describe life as dialectics with the world. We recognize this dialectics when we realize that the non-human world becomes *our* visual field when we see it, *our* aural world when we hear it, and so on for each of our external senses. In the totality of our existence one fundamental fact reveals itself: the world lends itself to interplay with man. This is quite obvious as a fact. But philosophical reflection upon it discovers a problem: how is it possible that the alien, the non-human lends itself to such an interplay or dialogue?

We would like to show the significance of this problem by means of a timely example, the dialogue between the physical sciences, including modern technology which has its roots in these sciences, and the world. Modern sciences make intensive use of mathematics. They speak, if we may use this expression, the language of mathematics. A publication on a strictly scientific level, not a popularization, usually contains a long series of mathematical formulae.

Mathematics, however, is the most constructive of all sciences.[5] In the philosophy of mathematics there is a controversy on the question of whether or not mathematics has its starting point in reality. The affirmative answer seems to be more probable, for the mathematician does not create quantity but simply finds it "already" given. Nevertheless, mathematics is not a reflection upon quantity as it occurs in our

---

[4] "Human existence is therefore a co-existence of individuals, which manifests a plurality of forms and structures. The interpretation which viewed society as one which emerges from the necessity of the individual to seek human cooperation for the satisfaction of his needs, is antiquated." Tellegen, *Zelfwording en zelfverlies in de arbeid,* Waltman, Delft, page 14.

[5] "Mathematics is in many respects a free creation of the human spirit, and more so than other sciences. This does not mean, however, that it is a science of the spirit (*Geisteswissenschaft*), for its object is not the human spirit." Andrew G. van Melsen, "De ontmoeting van natuur- en geesteswetenschappen," *Ontmoeting tussen natuur- en geesteswetenschappen,* Academisch Genootschap, Eindhoven, 1955, page 6.

experience. Before quantity could become the object of mathematics, the human mind had to travel the road of abstraction. No matter, however, what may be the starting point of mathematics, it is beyond dispute that this science is essentially very constructive. Mathematical quantities are creations of the intellect. Geometric figures and algebraic equations are the work of the human mind. Until recently Euclidean geometry strongly dominated mathematical science, but it is losing its monopoly. The creation and expansion of the mathematical realm continues to make progress. This realm has become so gigantic that a universal comprehension of the entire field by one man is almost impossible. The constructive nature of mathematics makes it a science in which we can best succeed in catching the movement of human thought. For this reason the science of logic, which is concerned with the movement of thought as such, has a close connection with mathematics.

The physical sciences, as we pointed out, utilize this constructive science of mathematics but, while so doing, they are also a dialogue with the world. They want to uncover inorganic nature and bring it to light. Scientists use human forms of thinking, but in these forms they speak about the realities of the world. We find ample evidence of this also in modern technology, which became possible through the physical sciences. Atomic submarines would not be able to cruise below the seas, if nuclear physics were not true knowledge of our physical world.

There arises a problem which comprises the whole of physical science and modern technology—namely, how is it possible that inorganic nature can be brought to light in *human* forms of thinking? How can human thought constructs elucidate nature? The physicist simply presupposes that it is possible. Contemporary physicists search for a formula which expresses the innermost nature of cosmic reality. This search presupposes that the whole of inorganic reality can be considered scientifically. If, as often happened, laboriously constructed systems revealed themselves inapplicable to certain realms of reality, scientists at once began to search for new formulae which would cover also these realms. The supposition that inorganic nature contains sectors which are beyond the reach of science is an hypothesis which is not even made by physicists. They simply presuppose that nature is knowable and, if necessary, could point to the success of technology to justify their presupposition. The problem, however, is, how is it possible that nature can be brought to light through constructive thinking, through mathematical formulae? The problem would disappear if we were to assume that physical science merely mirrors what is given or does not bring nature to light at all. But these assumptions do not agree with the facts. We are therefore faced with a paradox: man is involved in a dialogue with the world, and this non-human world lets itself be brought to light in *human* language.

These reflections indicate this problem in the realm of physical science, but the same problem exists in any realm in which man associates with nature. The vision of our eyes implies that the world becomes a field of vision, in which things appear with color and shape in a spatial whole. This is possible only because things are visible and thus lend themselves for interplay with man. The same problem appears also if we consider man in his work: things let themselves be penetrated by human meanings. When man composes or paints, it appears that the world can be expressed in sounds, colors, and lines.

It is somewhat difficult to ascend to the level of reflection on which this problem is located. But as soon as we arrive there, that which seemed a self-evident association of man with the world becomes very mysterious. One might attempt to eliminate the problem by saying that man is part of the world. Our embodiment integrates us with the world and together with our planet we move in the gigantic space of the cosmos. But our problem still stands, because man is involved in a dialogue with the world not as being a part of nature, but precisely as other than nature.

We touch here the most profound contradiction of Marxist philosophy. It is true that this philosophy is dialectic, insofar as it puts itself within the dialogue of man and world. But at the same time this dialectic approach is destroyed by its materialism. Marxism is based on the assumption that man is ultimately a part of the cosmos and that he is brought forth by nature, which then becomes a partner in the dialogue of nature and man. This is an internal contradiction, Marxism has only one choice: either it takes its dialectics seriously and abandons its crude materialism, or it takes its materialism seriously and disregards its dialectics. The fact that many philosophers have become aware of this contradiction has made Marxism unrealistic as a philosophy, although its many valuable elements cannot be disregarded.

Our problem comprises our total existence, our entire association with the world. Merleau-Ponty touches upon it again and again. For example, he says that metaphysical consciousness "discovers the fundamental strangeness of everything"[6]; and again he speaks about "the emergence of phenomena on all levels of the world and the continuous birth described by the philosopher."[7] Strangely enough, he refuses to see a problem in this fundamental fact of philosophy. This constitutes the weakness in his thought: he discovers a fundamental datum, but refuses to acknowledge its revealing power.

Furthermore, a unity within multiplicity reveals itself here. Contact between man and world, genuine dialectics, is conceivable only because of a certain opposition between man and world. But within this opposition there is unity, because the world lets itself be grasped by man in many ways, because the world lends itself to humanization. This unity in multiplicity is a fundamental problem of philosophy. The world

---

6   Maurice Merleau-Ponty, *Sens et non-sens*, Nagel, Paris, 1948, page 189.
7   Maurice Merleau-Ponty, *Eloge de la philosophie*, Gallimard, Paris 1953, page 62.

appears as a hidden light, a light submerged in darkness. If this were not so, this light would not let itself be brought forth. Plato understood it when he described the cosmos as a participation in the world of pure ideas. Aristotle envisioned it when he spoke about the potential intelligibility of the world. Hegel used a genial expression when he spoke of the world as "hidden spirit." The humanization of the world points to a hidden relationship of man and world which is presupposed in the totality of our existence.[8]

B. The Interhuman Encounter

The problem of unity in multiplicity becomes manifest, although in a different fashion, in the mutual encounter of people. Man has created a world of meaning through interhuman relationships and mutual contacts. The meaningful world is also the product of the human relationships and contacts of many former generations. The encounter of people, therefore, always takes place within a historical framework. Its nature may differ according to the differences of time and place. This is one of the reasons why a visit to far away countries is so appealing; we find there a different way of being-together and often an altogether different world. History also shows us that there are many and diverse ways of encounter and of being-together. We take these modes of encounter for granted, and the inter-human contact seems self-explanatory. Modern times have also brought revolutionary developments, increasing tremendously the possibilities of encounter. The use of the word "possibilities" here is insufficient; we should also refer to desirability and to necessity, because in the modern world, an extensive, world-wide network of communications has become a necessity. The industrial revolution has made it necessary, and technology has made it possible. For the first time in history the world has become a single large realm of encounter.

Because modern man during the short period of his own life experiences the creation of new modes of encounter, it is obvious that he is becoming strongly aware of the facticitous and historical nature of traditional modes of encounter. It is even more obvious because the mode of encounter between people is experienced also as a task and a subject of serious concern. We have developed the life of encounter so rapidly and so intensely that this development has become a problem,

---

[8] One could speak here of a fundamental problem of contemporary thinking. Since, thanks to the manifold development of labor, the relationship between man and the world clearly reveals its dynamic nature, the attention of philosophy could not fail to be drawn to it. Philosophical thinking, therefore, places itself more and more within a dialectic perspective. This is true for Marxism, existentialism as well as for phenomenology. Scholastic philosophy emphasizes the role of the agent intellect and stresses that human knowledge is an interplay of man and the world. However, it is striking that the question of the possibility of dialectics is rarely raised.

as appears from the necessity of special advisers in "human relations." We have made interhuman contacts so multiform that it has become increasingly difficult to experience them as authentic encounters. Relations are becoming impersonal to such a degree that they cause grave concern. Because we have witnessed the creative power of history, and because we realize at the same time that we are placed before a clearly defined task, we are aware, more profoundly than other generations, that the modes of encounter between people are the result of an historical development.

It is very easy, however, to exaggerate this point. One may come to regard the modes of encounter as purely facticitous and as being determined entirely by historical development. This position has far-reaching consequences. If actual history is regarded as the exclusive cradle of intersubjectivity and universality, it will lead to the conclusion that the universal character of meaning and truth is merely historical and consequently contingent. This point of view is defended by Merleau-Ponty.[9] Historical development supposedly brought people together, or rather within this historical development people are supposed to have found the road to one another. The intersubjective nature of truth, norms and customs would, in that case, be entirely the result of the converging movements of history. Even as art expresses the world in color, in lines, and in melody, and even as the meaning of a work of art is limited by the development of a pattern of expression, so also would intersubjective truth be limited by the history of the word.

Eternal and absolute truth would thus be inconceivable. For how would it be possible for absolute and eternal truth to emerge and live within contingent means of expression? True, verbal expression has some advantages over artistic expression. The former may be stored in memory, recorded in books and, therefore, may be reproduced over and over again. The incarnation of meaning in artistic expression, on the other hand, is as a rule unique and non-repeatable. Verbal expression, however, may be taken up by many at different times in such a way that there arise generally accepted and continuous modes of expression. Merleau-Ponty uses the term "sedimentation" for this process. Because of it, he claims, we may nurse the illusion of eternal and absolute truth, but in reality this so-called eternal and absolute truth is nothing else than what is acquired through centuries of historical development.[10]

Merleau-Ponty does not deny the intersubjectivity of truth and values, but he regards it as purely *de facto* and historical. We are never assured, he says, in an aprioristic way of our contact with others, but we must find the road to one another through an often laborious

---

[9] See especially his article "Le métaphysique dans l'homme," which is included in *Sens et non-sens*, pages 165-196.

[10] "L'intemporel, c'est l'acquis." What is considered supratemporal truth must still be regarded as humanly acquired truth. Maurice Merleau-Ponty, *Phénoménologie de la perception*, page 450.

historical development. For this reason no one has the right to regard his truth as truth for all. Its intersubjectivity must be realized within actual contact; a real dialogue is possible only if we are willing to be influenced by others.

Undoubtedly there is a considerable amount of truth in all this. The role of the actual encounter in our historical development is greater than could ever have been imagined in the past. Man, therefore, is tempted to indicate history as the producer of all encounters and of all norms of encounter. But this is going too far.

If we reflect, for example, upon the encounter of the sexes, we find that the way in which young couples become acquainted, their courtship and the preparation for marriage are determined historically. In some civilizations the young meet and after a period of courtship choose each other; in others their families arrange the marriage, sometimes even without consulting the prospective partners. Regardless, however, of these historically given modes of encounter, the sexes are driven towards each other by a force which is not the product of an historical development. When those who marry live together and beget children, they know that the mystery of life which takes place in them is given to man and not produced by him. There are here modes of encounter which vary and differ throughout history, but which are not mere products of this history.

Likewise, it is impossible to explain the intersubjectivity of truth only and exclusively as a product of historical development. We do not mean by this that there is a truth outside or above history. All truth blooms within the framework of history. But the power of truth is not entirely dependent upon history. There are many reasons which may seem to indicate the contingent nature of truth, but each individual reason and all the reasons together cannot destroy the remarkable claim of our judging intellect. When I judge, I accept a truth as a certainty. As long as there is still a shadow of doubt in my mind I can speak only of a presumption or of an opinion, but not of a judgment. But when I really judge, I accept and recognize a truth, which I recognize not as a truth just for myself, but a truth with validity for all. It is absolutely impossible for me to accept something as truth, and at the same time accept that this truth does not hold for others. If, for instance, someone would make the judgment that every pronouncement has relative value, then he would be convinced that this holds not only for his own pronouncements, but also for those of Aristotle, Plato, Kant, and Hegel. By making the judgment that all truth is relative, he affirms an absolute truth and destroys implicitly his own thesis. The testimony of our judging intellect will always kill any form of relativism. The absoluteness of the judgment of our intellect confirms itself even in the denial of absolute truth. One may wonder how insight and truth emerge within a contingent means of expression, such as the human word, but the fact that it does always forces itself upon us.

It is this fact which requires a more profound reflection. The individual who judges is always a particular subject, who partakes of a history, who stands in a particular place in the immense whole of time and space. He has a particular disposition and his own social heritage. His particularity implies that he is distinct from all other human subjects. In a word, the multiplicity of human subjects is an incontestable fact. Still, when this particular individual judges, he judges for all and in the name of all; he cannot do otherwise. In his individuality, he is at the same time universal. The many subjects are indeed numerous and yet they are innerly *one*. This unity cannot be reduced to mere *de facto* participation in the same historical development. Moreover, if truth were not universal, it would be exposed as simulated truth. If we can show that the thesis of a philosopher is the product of his personality, of his times, of other philosophers, or of his social environment, we show at the same time that his thesis lacks veracity.

The judging human subject, therefore, is particular and universal at the same time. He is universal in his particularity and particular in his universality. Again we have found a manifestation of that remarkable phenomenon, unity in multiplicity. This phenomenon, especially in connection with truth, prompted Kant to speak of "a transcendental subject," it inspired Hegel to speak of "the Spirit," and again of "the Subject," which reveals itself empirically in many subjects. There was a time when this viewpoint seemed very strange to the author of this book, but this is no longer the case. The universality of truth reveals to us a mysterious, inner unity in the multiplicity of human subjects. It is for this reason that Husserl calls the philosopher a "functionary of humanity": whoever takes philosophizing seriously should be aware of the fact that he is searching for truth in the name of, and for the benefit of humanity.[11]

3. Metaphysical Consequences

The way in which we discovered unity in multiplicity was twofold. The actual humanization of the world which takes place in any form of dialectics between man and world reveals to us that things lend themselves to humanization, to being brought to light. There is a hidden affinity between man and the infrahuman world. This affinity justifies Hegel's point of view that the world is hidden spirit. In human beings there exists a mysterious and inner unity within their multiplicity. The forms of unity in multiplicity become manifest within the realm of encounters developed by man. We are not speaking here about possible conditions hidden behind empirical reality, but about structural elements of our actual world. The affinity of man and the world manifests itself

---

[11] "It is impossible to overlook the fact that we are *functionaries of humanity*." Edmund Husserl, *Die Krisis der europäischen Wissenschaften und die transzendentale Phänomenologie, Husserliana VI,* Nijhoff, The Hague, 1954, page 15.

in every culture. The unity between the many human subjects is clearly apparent in philosophy and the sciences.

Should we not envision all this as an indication of the Absolute Spirit, of God? Unity in multiplicity is an indication of a single common origin. The striking unity in the plurality of subjects, the universality in human particularity signify that the many human individuals partake of one Absolute Spirit, who hovers above the multiplicity, yet reveals himself in it. The affinity of man and world also points to one origin and would be inconceivable if man as spirit and the world as hidden spirit did not spring from one source. Many questions, of course, arise here. For example, in what sense can we speak of a proof and of a conclusion? How do we elevate our thinking above worldly actuality?[12] But these questions are beyond the purpose of this book and particularly of this chapter, in which we wish merely to open a few perspectives.

The foregoing considerations disclose that "being," the object of metaphysics, must be understood as personal. What is first and foremost accessible to us is the "being" of persons. Through the encounter with human persons we become familiar with the infra-human. The way in which we have access to "being" is decisive for our concept of it. The question, sometimes asked in scholasticism, of what makes being become personal, seems therefore irrelevant.[13] The "being" which is first and foremost manifest to us, is already personal. The question is rather, what is the meaning of the impersonal being of the things? Is it not true that the infra-human world is accessible to us only insofar as it is humanized, in other words, when it is drawn within the human, the personal sphere? In the light of this view the non-human appears as an inferior form of being. We can exist with it, but it is a low degree of co-existence, not because of its hidden riches but because of its poverty. This poverty causes the infra-human world to be darkness for us to a great extent.

The metaphysical forms of thinking must be rethought along these

---

[12] We believe that we express a philosophical experience when we formulate the assertion that the critico-reflective justification of the progressive stages of thinking becomes more difficult as we approach the domain of the spirit. The conclusion "God exists" is, if one thinks within a certain perspective, inescapable and self-evident. But one who tries to justify critico-reflectively the "why" of this thought process easily finds himself confronted with an impasse. The thought process has apparently an analogous character. This analogy is disregarded in formal logic. Thus the question arises, whether formal logic, as we know it and especially as it is elaborated in symbolic logic, is not the logic of a particular plane of thinking, that is, of the univocal plane. It appears to us that the logical element of our life of thought is richer and more differentiated than the logic formulated in the science of formal logic. Consequently, a further question arises: may we subject the process of thinking toward God to the exigencies of our formal logic? Is there not a legitimate form of thinking possible which transcends the exigencies of our formal logic?

[13] "Distinctio inter naturam et subsistentiam est distinctio realis modalis." Josephus Gredt, *Elementa Philosophiae Aristotelicae-Thomisticae*, vol. II, page 131. Because personality lies in the line of "subsistence," there is a real and modal distinction between nature and personality.

lines. This rethinking, however, is already in process. The substance which we know primarily, and which is substance for us in its most striking sense, is precisely the person. He is a "self" who thinks and decides, who takes a viewpoint. If we wish to apply the idea of substance to the infra-human realm, we are in the dark; in the sphere of the inorganic world we no longer know when to speak of substance. Late scholasticism occupied itself too much with the thing-like realm, so that the metaphysical categories were rendered obscure.

The same is true for causality. Often causality has been presented as belonging *par excellence* to inorganic nature and hardly applying to the activity of man. We still find statements that, in the area of interhuman activity, we should not speak of causal relations. However, in the light of the metaphysical perspectives developed in this chapter, we should assume a different attitude. Causal activity is found in its fullest and proper sense within the personal encounter. When we talk with one another, love one another, work together or play together, in other words, when we really encounter one another, we cause each other to be. We all know from experience that the fullness of life is given to us supremely by our fellow man. He brings us light and joy, sorrow, and loneliness. We perfect one another even more by mutual love. Outside the sphere of love, life is really incomplete and even the highest values lose their attraction. Accordingly, we cause one another to be in many ways which are difficult to distinguish. Causality has here a fullness and an abundance which are indescribable.

When we use the term causality in the infrahuman realm, its significance weakens progressively as we recede from man. It is true that infrahuman causality precisely because of its weakened significance, is easier to lay down in concepts, but that does not mean that we are dealing with the idea of causality in its most actual and proper meaning.

If all this is taken into consideration, it becomes less strange to apply the idea of causality to God. Divine causality should not be envisioned as in line with thing-like causality, but rather in the line of man's causal activity. Human causality reaches its highest form in the gratuitous gift of self in love.

We would like to repeat again that we are not writing a new metaphysics, but merely are trying to sketch new metaphysical perspectives in line with the basic thesis of this book.[14] However, we are convinced that an acceptance of the primacy of the human encounter leads to a personalistic metaphysics which may throw new light upon some seemingly insoluble problems. For example, it will mean a breakthrough of Kant's impasse. Kant feels that metaphysics should be rejected, because in his

---

14 There is agreement between the views developed in this book and the article of E. Minkowski, "Co-existence et co-devenir," *Rencontre, Contributions à une psychologie humaine, dédiées au professeur F. J. J. Buytendijk*, Utrecht, 1957, pages 295-307. The article in question embodies a view which is not elaborated systematically.

opinion, there is only one perception which leads to true *"Erkentniss"* (knowledge), and that is sensory perception. As soon as we try to rise beyond sensory perception we are in a vacuum where no true *"Erkentniss"* is possible. However when we keep in mind that we are primarily familiar with human beings, with persons, and that human encounter is the mediating factor in knowledge of the infrapersonal, we have already transcended sense perception in our world of cognitive presence. We have entered the sphere of the "existent" spirit. It is an important task of contemporary philosophy to rethink the new light of this personalistic perspective on a metaphysical level.

CHAPTER SIX

ETHICAL PERSPECTIVES

Our fundamental thesis insists upon the social character of human existence. This social character has many implications. In general, people who understand their time have a feeling for these implications, but even they frequently fail to see clearly the foundations on which the implications are based. For this reason we must point out here the ethical perspectives that are opened up by the social character of man's life.

The preceding pages have shown that man's existence, insofar as it is authentically human, is in all respects a being-together. Our familiarity with the world is conditioned by this togetherness, for it is only within the encounter with our fellow men that we become familiar with the world. If, then, being-together is the fundamental sphere in which all human activities take place, it follows that it is also in this togetherness that we must seek our ethical ideals as well as the ultimate basis of disorder and sin.

1. The Anonymity of Human Togetherness

In order to understand the implications which are involved here, we should recall that the being-together of man is deeply submerged in anonymity. It is submerged in an almost thing-like atmosphere which is so much taken for granted that it escapes our attention and remains nameless ("anonymous" means having no name). Our being-together takes place in the world of today, the world in which *things* have become of greatest importance, often over and above that of human beings.

We have said that our association with things is conditioned by the encounter with our fellow men. We might reverse this statement and say, that we encounter one another by working together in this world. Actually this is not entirely true, because we may seek being-together for togetherness' sake; but ordinary, everyday encounter takes place in our common activity in the world. As a consequence the entire constellation of the human world is permeated with the encounter between people. The way in which we have built a thing-like human world reflects the mode in which we live together. Our being-together has assumed, as it were, a thing-like face. If we reverse this thought, we may say that the world as we have made it today, forces us into a particular way of being-together.

If we wish to learn about the way in which people are together, it might suffice to look into their homes. The small farmhouse in the country is usually functional; it reflects an atmosphere of working together. The homes of city dwellers, who have their work away from home, are first and foremost places of relaxation and of pleasant being-together. It is impossible to live together in the city in the same informal and simple way as country folks do. Also, the way in which a road is built indicates how people use it. The streamlined turnpikes and thruways, their lack of regard for preserving the landscape point to man's hurry to move about quickly. Such roads do not invite us to take a walk. The winding country road and the way in which it is part of the landscape, reflects a completely different pace of life; it indicates a way of life which is much more closely interwoven with nature.[1] The world in which we are born, forces us to be together with our fellow men in a definite fashion.

The same idea reveals itself in the interior of a factory or of an office. The arrangement of the machinery or of the equipment implies a certain way of working together. For instance, the production line indicates the speed with which work is done and a particular mode of working together. Here also interhuman relationships are embodied in things. If one compares the cafeteria of a French factory with that of a modern American industrial plant, one can see that in the United States much more attention is paid to the well-being of the laborer during his lunch hour. One could start a study of interhuman relations in factories by inspecting the working space, considered as expression of a human encounter.

Briefly, we may say that the way in which we build our homes, construct our cities and villages, the way in which we extend a network of highways all over the country, and arrange our factories, all this reflects a particular mode of human encounter. Today's world of things is a product and a manifestation of this particular mode of encounter. Our existence and co-existence are to a certain extent interwoven with this humanized world.

Human relations also are anonymously and somewhat less visibly embodied in ownership and property. The fact that I can call a little piece of the world my own means that it does not belong to someone else. The fence around an estate, the barbed wire around a piece of farmland, limit the freedom of other people. The anonymous mode of being-together is reflected also in large apartment buildings erected close to a slum-ridden area.

Our modes of being-together are embodied also in our everyday social behavior. This too belongs to the anonymous sphere in which we grow up and live, without having chosen it consciously and personally. There is a certain manner in which the employee addresses his employer, the patient his doctor, the driver a policeman, the child his teacher etc. As a matter of fact, the child is actually born into a particular social

---

[1] Concerning this point consult the interesting article of J. Linschoten, "Die Strasse und die unendliche Ferne," *Situation, Beiträge zur phänomeno-logischen Psychologie und Psychopathologie,* Utrecht, 1954, pages 235-260.

position and the code of conduct that goes with it. Being-together has always certain forms which cannot be changed easily, not even in our days of fast progress.[2]

The way in which people are together in a church is implied by the interior of the church building. In Spanish churches, for instance, the space for the clergy is rigorously separated from that of the faithful, which indicates a striking dissociation. The front pews for the wealthy bourgeois and the back pews for the poor, an arrangement still found in certain European churches, points to a particular set of human relations even within the church building.

Law also is rooted in this anonymity and consequently is permeated with it. Laws are the expression not only of ethical ideals, but also of current patterns of common behavior. A change in laws is almost always preceded by a change in human relations. The compelling force behind the structure of law is partially a confirmation of current social conduct, and as such, law becomes an expression of the above-mentioned anonymity. There is therefore a certain amount of self-deception in the position of the economic and sociological sciences when they attempt to be purely positive and not normative. Certainly, economy and sociology are confronted with an economic and social world which is an actuality and can be approached as such. But this actuality is, so to speak, thing-like, solidified humanity. This *de-facto*-being-so is not in the same way as "a stone is a stone," but is permeated with human intentions of which we are no longer aware.[3] The total facticitous character of the world order in which we live is not on an objective neutral level but on a *moral level*. This world order is, therefore, morally good or morally bad, worthy of man or unworthy of him. Moreover, the anonymous facticitous order invites us to participate in it. It wants to integrate us into itself and asks us to continue it. By accepting this invitation, we promulgate and prolong this order, whether good or evil.

---

[2] This is evident from the relatively slow rise of the lower social classes. In principle, any profession is open to any talented child, but in fact the low social status of an adolescent who goes to college is often a handicap. The facts indicate that not only the intellectual but also and especially the social ability is of importance. (The author refers here to a specifically European condition. In the United States the social differences between the classes are often no handicap at all in a similar situation.—Note of the translator.)

[3] Merleau-Ponty correctly calls the petrified and thing-like mode of human existence a kind of second nature. A person living in it easily sees it as something self-evident. Thus there is danger that he will begin to speak of it as "a natural order." If he regards God as the origin of nature, he will ultimately impute this solidified human character to God. An enumeration of everything which in the course of history has been attributed to God in this fashion would fill several volumes. The result is that man often has a distorted image of God. As Dostoevski remarks in his book *The Brothers Karamazov,* the pious are often responsible for atheism because they present a wrong image of God. As Christians, we have the privilege of representing The Absolute in history. We therefore must be on guard against the tendency to relativize the absolute. Likewise, we must be careful not to abuse The Absolute to absolutize the relative.

2. *The Personal Level in the Anonymous Order*

There is, of course, also a personal level. The same anonymous order may be taken up differently by different people. For instance, we are well convinced now that the capitalistic order of the last century was grossly evil and inhuman. But within this inhuman capitalistic order, there were good and bad capitalists. Likewise, slavery was an inhuman institution, but there were good and bad masters. The social norms of past centuries reflected an unnatural distance between the classes of population; but they were not *always* abused. In other words, the anonymous sphere does not fully determine the personal moral attitudes; but there is an important margin of freedom and there are many different ways of human response to the same anonymous order. Saints and criminals are possible in any such order.[4] The best order does not guarantee the goodness of the individual, just as the worst order does not mean that every individual is evil.

Therefore, we should make a distinction between the anonymous and the personal level, between the anonymous order and the way in which an individual assimilates it. The two levels intermingle. The personal level exists only as the taking-up of the anonymous order, and the anonymous order continues to exist because it is taken up in a personal fashion. In both spheres, that of the anonymous and that of the personal, our existence is a being-together. The anonymous order which makes our personal existence possible is social by nature, and this reason suffices to place our personal existence on a social level.

We touch here a problem of contemporary ethics which is of the greatest importance. It is the problem of the relation between the anonymous and the personal level. The best way to illustrate it, is to make a comparison between Marxist and Catholic morality. (We refer here to the Catholic morality expressed in the manuals of moral theology of a recent past.)

Marxism divides the world of man into an infrastructure and a superstructure or, as we have said before, a lower level and an upper level. The infrastructure consists of the economic-industrial aspect of life taken as a human way of existence. This aspect is found in the way in which people work together to cultivate the world. The superstructure consists of the other aspects of life. Marxism puts all emphasis on the infrastructure and claims that the latter determines the superstructure. In the words of Karl Marx himself:

> What is a society, whatever its form may be? It is the product of mutual human contact. Are people free to choose this or that form of society? Not at all. Given a certain phase in the development of the productive powers of the populations, a corresponding

---

[4] Marxism is blind to this, because it thinks entirely infrastructurally. Sartre, Simone de Beauvoir, and originally also Merleau-Ponty, in their articles on social subjects, reveal that they have been influenced onesidedly by Marxism.

form of trade and of consumption will result. Given a certain phase in the development of production, trade, and consumption, a corresponding social structure, a corresponding organization of family life, of social classes, a corresponding civil society will be the result. Given such a society, the result will be a corresponding political situation, which is nothing else but the official expression of society.[5]

We call this an "infrastructural" way of thinking. For the infrastructural way of thinking the personal attitude is merely a concomitant phenomenon. Whether one is morally good or bad depends on the infrastructure. A capitalist is bad because he is a capitalist. He is an exploiter and lives from someone else's labor. The fact that he personally may be a nice man, a man who is good to his employees, and treats them well, does not matter in the least. For Marx, all questions and problems are decided by the infrastructure.

This viewpoint contains both the value and the weakness of Marxism. Value, because Marxism does not take for granted the existence of the infrastructure, but tries to analyze and understand it. It postulates the possibility that the constituted order of law and justice in reality may not be just at all. It postulates the possibility that the anonymous way of being-together in society is, in fact, inhuman. Marxism critically investigates the structure of society. It is not misled by the fact that these structures are proclaimed as the natural order, but examines them without mercy. In the last century this was a revolutionary way of thinking and even today, it is of great importance. But the weakness of the Marxist system is that it regards as purely concomitant and accidental the personal existence, the way in which a person accepts the infrastructure.

Catholic morality, as expressed in the theological manuals of the recent past, was too exclusively concerned with the personal realm. It based itself on innate laws of nature; it was an appeal to a personal conscience. This kind of morality regarded the personal attitude as decisive, and occupied itself chiefly with personal ethics.

It is true that there was also a social aspect, because it recognized charity as the highest moral law and the greatest commandment, but still charity was regarded principally as a personal moral virtue. The strength of Catholic morality lays in the formation of conscience and the appeal to a personal morality, its weakness in the little attention paid to anonymous existence, the infrastructure. It is in vain that one seeks in these manuals for a judgment regarding the morality of the anonymous structures current in the times in which they were written. One gets the impression that these anonymous structures were accepted as self-evident with hardly any criticism or comment.

This was a serious shortcoming, because the anonymous sphere of

---

[5] Karl Marx, *Brief an Annenkow*, Brussel 28 Dec., (*Das Elend der Philosophie*, Dietz Verlag, Berlin, 1957, page 6).

institutions and interrelationships is a human edifice and consequently, embodies moral values. This sphere cannot be simply taken for granted, but should be judged from the viewpoint of morality. The objection could be raised that the function of ethics is to lead the personal conscience and that, therefore, it is not concerned with the anonymous sphere. The reply to this is contained in the preceding paragraphs: the personal attitude is the way of taking up social and anonymous existence and, therefore, is permeated with the moral value of the anonymous social sphere.

A doubt could be raised about the truth of this statement. One could say that anonymous existence is so submerged in darkness that it lies outside the domain of moral responsibility. The answer is that anonymous existence is neither entirely light nor entirely darkness, but it is wrapped in the semi-darkness of twilight. Although there may be less moral responsibility because of the obscurity of our awareness and the relative freedom of willing acceptance there still is awareness and freedom and, consequently, also responsibility. Christian morality, therefore, must think also in terms of the infrastructure.

Our time is beginning to become aware of this infrastructural morality.[6] The anonymous structures are changing so rapidly that they cannot avoid attracting attention. Christians are becoming conscious of the moral problems existing in this realm. There are moral questions in the realm of trade, traffic, the stock market, and colonialism.

Of course, there is no doubt that the Christian regards Marxist thinking with disapproval. Marxism neglects the dimension of personal choice in relation to existence. The Gospel calls for a personal moral attitude, and this is exactly what Marxism ignores and considers as incidental. According to the Gospel, man may be a saint or an evildoer in any social order. Speaking of the Last Judgment, Christ says: "Two women will be grinding together; one will be taken, and the other will be left. Two men will be in the field; one will be taken, and the other will be left."[7] Marxism neglects this sphere of essential Christian concern.

Although it is the task of Christianity to emphasize strongly the personal sphere of responsibility, it should nevertheless focus more attention upon the morality of the infrastructure. It should beware of confusing the existing structures too readily with the natural order or with the eternal order of God. We should also face the possibility that what is regarded as just, may be actually unjust and what seems a lawful demand may be in fact inhuman. This certainly heightens the responsibility of the Christian, but he may not shun it.

---

[6] An example of Christian thinking which takes into account the infrastructure is given by M. G. Plattel in his article "Bezitsvorming, sociaal-wijsgerige beschouwingen," *Sociale wetenschappen,* vol. I, no. 1, pages 3-20.

[7] St Luke 17 : 34-36.

3. *The Moral Responsibility for the Anonymous Order*

Only when we survey the full extent of the moral domain, do we understand how much every disorder is a disturbance of man's being-together and how far-reaching are the demands of love. The encounter of man and nature is effected within the mutual encounter of men. The entire, so-called, objective world of trade and transportation, of production, and means of production, in brief the world of labor, has come about through the encounter of men. The meaningful world in which we live, the world in which we see, hear and speak, the world in which we develop science is at the same time an encounter between people.

We may therefore describe the evolution of this human world as the development of a field of encounter. This description extends to all aspects of life and the world. In the history of this development two aspects always interlock—namely, the encounter between men and the establishment of a field of encounter. Thus, for example, the development of machinery in the world of industry is the development of the human encounter in the realm of labor. We could present examples from every sector of human existence. Neither aspect has a priority of time over the other, since the encounter is realized in the world, and this world as the field of encounter does not exist before the encounter itself. We may therefore describe the history of culture as the develop ment of man's being-together.

Christianity, as incarnation of the divine Word, teaches that charity is the constitutional law which must dominate the world of encounter. In this way the law of love should become the fundamental law of human history. It should dominate every aspect of man's world of encounter. Charity should obtain objective form in the anonymous sphere of existence, in the institutions, in the planning of industrial workshops, in the organization of the economic, social and political life. Charity should be the driving power of historical development. Every disorder in the human world would thus be attributed to immaturity of charity or to the absence of charity. Every real progress would mean a new incarnation of charity.

The realization of charity has two aspects. Charity must become reality both in anonymous existence and in the way this existence is personally taken up. What is surprising here is that the latter does not have to wait for anonymous existence in order to become charitable. In a world order without charity, man may exist in charity personally, although often not without heroic effort. During the time of slavery, a master had an absolute right over his slave, but there were masters who, inspired by Christianity, lived in a much more charitable relationship with their slaves than that which some of the modern plant-managers have with their employees in this era of social progress. There have been saints who practiced the virtue of charity to a high degree in all historical periods, and there are uncharitable persons in the most perfect social order. The objective realization of charity in the social order does not guarantee that a man will personally live a life of charity. Marxism does not know these paradoxes of personal charity in an uncharitable order and personal lack of charity in a charitable order, because it reduces the person to the realm of the anonymous.

In our time more emphasis must be laid upon the realization of charity in anonymous existence. It was Marx who claimed that economic development dominates history, because in our time there has been a very rapid economic evolution, the momentum of which has swept along with it all other aspects of life. This has not always been the case. There have been periods of history in which decisive events happened and yet, there were no proportionate changes in the economic infrastructure. The entrance of Christianity into the world is a striking example. The periods of the Reformation and the Enlightenment likewise cannot be explained from the economic infrastructure, at least not to the extent which Marxism would have us believe.

We can understand, nevertheless, how Marx arrived at his thesis. In his time the infrastructure exercised indeed a great and often decisive influence. In taking his own time as standard, Marx committed the error of believing that he had discovered a universal law for the whole of history. But we are still living in a period in which economic development dominates and shapes everything else. Many familiar institutions, such as the close family unit, colonial relationships and the sovereign state, are disappearing. Familiar structures, such as the employer-employee relation, the village community, the supremacy of the white race, are slowly withering away. New structures of world-wide scope are coming into existence. A rapid revision of existing law is in progress. Evidently, in such a time the realization of charity demands everyone's attention.

A relatively new phenomenon is the fact that the anonymous structures no longer arise in an unconscious or semiconscious fashion. Scientific planning increases daily in the world. We have moved from a freely evolving economy to a more scientifically guided and planned economy. The social sciences are trying to guide and plan the growth of human society. Even the designing of a home is no longer the result of free imagination or of following traditional patterns. It is becoming more and more a matter of highly rational and functional planning, often on a citywide, nationwide or even international level.

These planned structures will eventually submerge again into anonymity, but the fact of the planning itself signifies that man feels a responsibility for the total world of tomorrow. In our age the religion of charity should focus more attention than ever on the realization of charity in structures and institutions. The possibilities for its success are greater than ever, because of the fact that many people possess a sincere spirit of humanism.

It is not enough for the Christian to concentrate on the realization of charity in his personal existence and in his own intimate circle. Actually, if he merely does this, he is personally wrong because, if he understands the spirit of his time, he should know, merely by listening to his personal conscience, that a much broader task awaits him. He must take part in the organization of a new world, in proportion to his talents. The Christian should be present in the international organizations which will shape the world of tomorrow. A ghetto-attitude is more dangerous than ever, because Christianity would look foreign and archaic to the people of the future, and the role of charity would diminish. The Christian should not foster a feeling of distrust towards the humanism of non-Christians, on the pretext that non-Christians do not have supernatural charity. How indeed, would he know that this is the case? In making such a judgment, he would be guilty of neglecting the commandment of Christ not to judge.

Instead of segregating himself, the Christian should congregate in order to show others the implications and exigencies of genuine humanism. More than ever is man responsible for his world, and the Christian should fully participate in this responsibility. In the past mankind existed in scattered, isolated groups of nations, while politics acted as coordinating factor. But now this isolation is rapidly vanishing, and we are being integrated into a single great world order. The function of world politics is becoming more important every day, because it is emerging as the only means of controlling this world order. Whether we want to or not, we no longer live isolated in a small part of the world. We live in the *one* world which is organized by man. We all have an obligation to work together for this new world of man.

This does not mean that all specifically Catholic organizations are outmoded. In certain circumstances it may be desirable for us to cooperate as a group. Moreover, it is practically impossible to break abruptly with the past and, secondly, there may be local conditions which make specifically Catholic organizations a more effective instrument in building up the new world. But the presence of the Christian in the process of building a new world should be the primary concern and, if this concern demands a withdrawal from isolation, we should not hesitate to sacrifice even a splendid isolation.

The problems with which we are faced are of frightening magnitude. Events progress in such rapid succession that less than ever before may we depend upon lessons from the past. The effect of all this is to make our era rather difficult but at the same time exceedingly attractive.

Briefly put, Christian ethics, because it regards charity as its greatest commandment, is *par excellence* social. Christian morality demands that charity be incarnated into the structures of life. The realization of this aim cannot be brought about without thinking about the infrastructure. Charity demands that we actively participate in the rapid evolution of new world structures.

4. *Application of These Ideas to a Few Concrete Problems*

Science. Any pursuit of science is, as we have seen, a participation in a collective dialogue, and specialized science is a more refined dialogue between human beings. It follows, therefore, that the pursuit of science lies on an ethical level, and this not merely in an accidental fashion. For in every encounter or dialogue the attitude toward the other plays an important role. The pursuit of science requires openness toward others and willingness to communicate the results of one's research. This willingness is not something exceptional but a regular social obligation. For the scientist is able to make a discovery only because of the collective dialogue, and his individual discovery contributes to the continuation of the collective dialogue.

Unfortunately, the openness of the dialogue is often obstructed by economic and political factors which place men in opposition to one another. In that case there is no real encounter. This is the case particularly in our age in which science, through its encounter with labor, often plays an important role in the economy and the political struggle for power. This struggle often makes science subject to an arbitrary external power, and this situation does not agree with the social nature of science. The scientist may experience this situation as unethical.

The scientist should also draw the correct consequences from the fact that precisely in his pursuit of science he is dependent on society. He should realize that in his scientific work he owes a debt to society. The fact that his science is clearly defined and determined, the fact that he has excellent instruments for his research, the fact that a highly developed scientific language is at his disposal, all these are the fruits of a long, historically developed, human dialogue.

From these facts it follows that society has certain claims on the scientist and may avail itself of these claims. The scientist pursues his task on the basis of the historical and common achievements of society, and society cannot continue its life and function unless it avails itself of its claim on the achievements of its scientist-members. For this reason the scientist may not appeal to the exalted nature of his knowledge and to the necessity of science in today's world to secure for himself a social and economic status which goes far beyond that of other leaders of society. For he is merely a participant in a dialogue originated by society and not the sole fountain head from which the science springs which he pursues. There still are groups in society whose economic status lies considerably below that of others, although their contribution to the life of society is equally or even more important than that of groups which enjoy a higher economic status. A typical example is provided by the low salaries with which such a highly advanced technological society as the United States remunerates most of its college and university professors.

Family Life. In our days, problems in family life have come to the foreground. They, too, belong to the domain of social ethics. The inner life of the family is an integral form of encounter of high standing. Sexual life, therefore, must be viewed as an integral encounter between husband and wife. This viewpoint should serve also as a basis for the formulation and the understanding of the ethical principles concerning marital life. Elimination of the aspect of encounter from marital life through callous egoism is a greater moral evil than acts of procreation which are organically frustrated through contraception. In the same light we should also consider celibacy. It entails sacrificing the elevated, deeply human life of encounter in which husband and wife find their physical and spiritual completion and become more fully human. It would be unsocial to defend celibacy by depreciating the married state of life.

There are many complaints about modern family life. It has been said that the family of today is no longer a closely knit unit in which life and activities are centered in the home. We should realize, however, that the wonderful comforts, the effective home appliances, the many means to take part in cultural life, such as musical instruments, books, radio and television, are all things which we possess thanks to society. Because of the developments of technology and industry, the family of today has at its disposal many useful things which did not exist in the past. It should be clearly understood that our modern technological society can offers these things only thanks to the services of those who profit by it. Because the society offers much to the family, it will also ask more of the individual members of the family.

These two aspects must be viewed in connection with each other, otherwise we will not understand why the family of today should be "open," and why it is impossible to go back to the secluded family atmosphere of a nearby past. Thus we understand why at an early age the child has to leave the family home for many hours of the day to obtain an education. This education prepares the child to be a useful member of society and to take part in the often highly complicated dialogue which is in process in the world of today. The father, and sometimes also the mother, are often absent from the family home for long periods of time, because society has need of their services. The family also is subject to the rule, that he who benefits from society must subject himself to its exigencies, provided these exigencies do not go too far.

We hope that these few examples demonstrate what is meant when we say that life should be regarded as encounter. If with this idea in mind one studies the traditional manuals of morality, it will become clear that several of their chapters are urgently in need of revision.

CHAPTER SEVEN

THEOLOGICAL PERSPECTIVES

The viewpoints which have been developed in the preceding chapters are not without importance for theology. The author is no theologian by profession and therefore does not venture to present a theological exposition. Nevertheless, for the sake of completeness it may be useful to indicate briefly the theological implications of his theses.

1. The Social Character of Religion

The central theme of this book is that we are familiar primarily with our fellow men; through contact with them, we become familiar also with things. We have demonstrated abundantly the way in which within the human encounter we become familiar with the infrahuman world. We ought to realize however, that the human encounter does not familiarize us with the world only by way of initiation, but that it is a continuing process. This thesis must be extended also to the superhuman sphere. Through our encounter with people, we become familiar with and learn to know God. Religious life is by its very nature also a social reality. By using the word "social" here, we do not mean that religion requires a charitable attitude towards our fellow men. It is true that whoever acknowledges God as the common Father of all mankind must logically regard everyone as his brother. But if we use the word "social" in this context, we wish to indicate the fact that, because of our encounter with people, we come into contact with God. We will find God only in a community of people.

The individualism of a recent past regarded religion as a private affair. This individualism has not yet vanished completely. There are still people who think that they should not give a religious concept of life to their children, but that the child should make up his own mind and choose when he has become an adult. He should be "free" to formulate his own point of view on the problems of life. We cannot emphasize too strongly that anyone who takes this standpoint misjudges the true nature of our human existence. We become familiar with the infrahuman as well as with the superhuman through our encounter with others. Just as we cannot become familiar with the world through completely individual efforts, so is it impossible for the human individual to arrive all by himself at the acceptance of religion as the highest human value in life. We are destined to realize our existence within intersubjective contact. The study of history reveals to us that man, primitive man as well as civilized man, comes to religious life within a religious community of men.

Thus it becomes understandable that when God wanted to draw man toward Himself, He began by establishing a religious society. Although all kinds of possibilities were available to the Almighty, He respected His own creation. This does not mean, of course, that God was bound by anything else for He binds Himself only to His own plan of creation. This idea is usually expressed by saying that divine grace does never destroy nature, but builds upon it.

God wanted to draw mankind to Himself by entering history in person. Christ is God, God became man, and henceforth it is possible to encounter God in the human appearance of Christ. It is through Christ that God established on earth a community of people who believe and pray as a community. The generations after Christ can find God within this community and because of this community, which is traditionally called "the Church." The Church is the praying community of believers, in which man is in contact with God. As through being-together we become familiar with the world, so also do we become familiar with God within the Church.

However, this familiarity can be attained only if God really lives in the Church. If the Church were only a human community, which would believe in Jesus Christ as the revealing God and which would possess the word of God in the Bible, but which would be otherwise purely human, then there would be no guarantee that we encounter God in the Church. It is therefore in perfect concordance with the social nature of man that God not only became man in Christ but that He continues His incarnation in the Church. The incarnation of God means that God has entered human history and continues to live in it. The Church is therefore an institution of God, which is protected by the Spirit of God against errors of faith and morals. It is also an infallible institution because it is permeated with the presence of God.

2. *The Catholic and the Protestant View of the Church*

Since the Reformation there has been a deep fundamental difference between Catholic and Protestant theology on this point. Both groups agree that fallen man cannot encounter God in spirit and in truth unless God condescends and reveals Himself. Both consider Christ as God Incarnate, both agree that the word of God is contained in the Bible, which has divine authority. But when it comes to the continuation of God in the human history, then they go separate ways. The Reformation maintains that God has appeared once and for all in Christ and in the word of the Bible. The latter embodies all authority and is sufficient for all people of all times. There are of course many churches, but they have no other task than to pass on the word. They have authority only to preach the word of God. These churches embody the presence of God insofar as the absolute word of Scripture lives in them. The Spirit of God, it is true, works in human history but only by opening the hearts of men to the word of God in the Bible.

The Catholic Church, however, regards the appearance of God in the Incarnation and in the word of Scripture as a beginning, which is being continued unto the consummation of the world, because God continues to appear *in His Church*. There is no moment in history which marks the end of the epiphany of the Lord. It continues to permeate history. The Church is thus the community of God, established by Christ, enlightened by the word of the Bible and ever diffused throughout of the Spirit of Christ. Man encounters God simply by beginning to live in the Church. Certainly, this Church cannot teach and rule arbitrarily, she must remain faithful to the word of Revelation. This faithfulness is always threatened by man's narrow-mindedness and pride, but the presence of the Spirit of Jesus Christ is a guarantee that the Church will remain faithful to her essential fundamentals. The believer meets God simply by living in the Church, by thinking and by praying with her and in her.

Is it fitting for a Christian to criticize the Church? As could be expected, the Catholic answer will be different from that of the Protestants. The Protestant, in principle, attributes to himself the right, based upon the absolute authority of the word of God in the Bible, to judge and criticize the churches. These churches are ruled by a norm, which is the word of God. In the light of this word of God, the Protestant may accept or reject the churches. The Protestant, in principle, accepts his Church in the light of the Bible.

The Catholic, on the other hand, does not have the authority to judge his Church unqualifiedly. The living presence of the Spirit of Christ is a guarantee for him that his Church, in her essential structure, in her sacramental life, and in her doctrine on faith and morals, is the work of God and not the work of man. In this respect his Church is above criticism and thus he knows that he should believe her. It is true, however, that the life of the Church is in many respects also the work of man. Canon law is almost entirely a human creation. The actual organization of the care of souls is the result of human endeavors. The many church organizations are not divine institutions. The liturgical splendor which surrounds the administration of the sacraments is to a large extent of human design. Many practical ecclesiastical problems are solved by human management. This human management is naturally subject to human failure and shortsightedness, and thus affords an area for critical reflection. The Catholic, therefore, may judge that perhaps it would be better if the Church would be modified in certain respects.[1] However, there are structural elements in the visible Church which are above criticism. The defined doctrine concerning faith and morals may not be criticized, but should be accepted.

---

[1] See the valuable book of Karl Rahner, *Free Speech in the Church*, New York, 1960.

3. *The Church and the Ambiguity of Man*

We are not attempting to present here a theological treatise of the Church, but speak from a philosophical perspective. It seems to us that the Catholic viewpoint of the Church is more in harmony with the thesis developed in this book. Man becomes familiar with his world through being-together. It is therefore in concordance with the social nature of man, with his dependence on togetherness, that he encounter God within the community of a Church which embodies God's presence in the history of man. It is in harmony with his entire existence that he becomes familiar with God within his familiarity with a Church. Of course, there is no question here of a proof, for it is impossible to prove a theological viewpoint on a philosophical basis. But nevertheless, the philosopher is permitted to indicate a harmony, an analogy between his philosophical viewpoint and a datum of faith.

Moreover, it seems to us that in Protestant circles practice differs from doctrine. Perhaps there are a few Protestants who, with the word of God as their criterion, judge, criticize, and abandon the Church in which they were raised from childhood. But the vast majority encounter God in their Church, and they interpret the Bible as read and explained in their Church. Within their Church they learn to speak with God. For otherwise, how can one explain the continuity of adherence to the different Churches? The words "the Faith of our Fathers" expresses a social reality.

The Reformation was born in part, as a protest against the human element in the Church, manifesting itself in corruption and abuses. The Protestants wanted, therefore, to raise God, Christ, and the word of Revelation above human frailty. They, therefore, strongly emphasized man's sinfulness and God's transcendence. It was difficult for the Reformation to accept God's incarnation into a human society and to accept also that God allows man to encounter Him in an impure and defiled society of men. For this reason it raised the encounter with God, with Christ and with the Spirit to spiritual heights, transcending the sinful human community of the Church. God in His divine absoluteness remains above the history of man and, as a consequence, does not become incarnate, in the strict sense of the term, in a living community of men.

The Catholic, on the contrary, finds himself in an ambiguous situation. On the one hand, he regards his Church as an epiphany of God and as being through God's grace, beyond error. The Church itself is for him a mystery of faith. On the other hand, he observes within his Church, human weakness, human narrow-mindedness, corruption and sin. His Church is the appearance of God in human history, and yet priests and faithful must confess their guilt before they approach the Banquet of the Lord. Every Christian must say the prayer taught by the Lord,

"Forgive us our trespasses as we forgive those who trespass against us." Nevertheless, he believes that God lives in his human Church.

All meaning, all values, all norms and all forms of knowledge come to us through being-together, through the encounter with people. Being-together in society means the realization of values, but the values are always intermixed with non-values. The society of God, the Church, is part of the world which is the society of mankind; it must therefore also share in its ambiguity.

EPILOGUE

In this book a single fundamental thesis has been developed. We have demonstrated that we are familiar primarily with our fellow men and that within this primary familiarity we become acquainted with infrahuman and superhuman realities. This book, therefore, is a plea for the social nature of human existence. That man is social is, of course, not a particularly new assertion for it has always been considered one of man's many characteristics. However, profound reflection manifests that the social nature of man is not just one of the many human features, but is *the* central characteristic. Encounter is a "primitive fact,"[1] the "central reference-point," in the light of which man must be approached. We have shown that the world of labor, the sciences, metaphysics and ethics gain when they are seen in this perspective.

We are convinced that we have given expression to something which exists in the lives and the thinking of our contemporaries. This book could not have been written in the last century. It is the task of the philosopher to bring to light and to transform into explicit knowledge whatever lives in our minds and hearts in a preconscious state. We foster the hope that the reader feels that he has known all the time what is written in this book. The readers and the author are living in the same world. An author writes well, if the reader discovers himself in his work.

---

[1] Cf. Albert Dondeyne, *Contemporary European Thought and Christian Faith*, Pittsburgh, 1958, pages 5 and 39-40.

INDEX OF NAMES

INDEX OF SUBJECT MATTER

Interhuman, see *Communication, Encounter, Relations.*

KNOWLEDGE, of things and of man, 3 ff.; of man, 15; has no intermediary 18; origin of, 16, 25 ff.

LABOR, and language, 46.
Language, a social possession, 11; embodiment of thought, 19, 41; thinking of a nation embodied in, 41; is human encounter, 42; and labor, 46. See also *"Word," Thought.*
Law, and the anonymous existence, 67; Canon, 79.
Logic, science of, 55; formal, 61.

MAN, embodied consciousness, 37.
Marxism, 7, 28, 30; and being-together, 33 f.; and the Catholic theologian, 42; and metaphysics, 52; unorthodox, 53; contradictory philosophy, 54; and dialectics, 57; morality of, and Catholic morality, 68 ff.; weakness of, 69 f.; and charity, 72.
Materialism, 6 f.; 52, 56.
Mathematics, the grasping potencies of language greatest in, 46 f.; not more familiar with the object of, than with man, 48; philosophy of, 48, 54; and reality, 54 f.
Metaphysics, 12, 51 ff,; possibility of, 51 f.; and encounter, 53 f.; personalistic, 62.
Morality, see *Catholic, Ethics, Marxism.*
Multiplicity, unity in, 56 f.; 60.

"NATURAL ATTITUDE," according to Husserl, 8 f.
Nihilism, 45.
Nominalism, 35.

PHENOMENOLOGY, 8, and dialectics, 57. See also *Husserl, Merleau-Ponty* (in Index of Names).

Physics, the object of, 46.
Planning, scientific, 72.
Politics, function of world, 73.
Positivism, 52.
Protestant, theologian and Catholic theologian, 42; and Catholic view of the church, 78 ff. See also *Reformation.*
Psychology, of consciousness, 4 f.; Gestalt, 5.

RATIONALISM, and the origin of knowledge, 16, 26 ff.; Merleau-Ponty's protest against, 40.
Reformation, 78, 80. See also *Protestant.*
Relations, interhuman, 12, 15, 18. See also *Encounter, Communication.*
Relationship, with-the-world, 27 f.
Relativism, 52 f.
Religion, 1, its social nature, 77 f.

SCHOLATICISM (Late), 1, 57; and word, 35; and personal being, 61; too much occupied with the thing-like realm, 62; and the distinction between the sciences, 43.
Sciences the, modes of human encounter, 43 ff.; distinction between the, 43; as collective dialogue, 49; physical, and metaphysics, 52; dialogue with the world, 54 ff.; and mathematics, 55; and ethics, 74.
Scientist, and ethics, 74.
Sexual life, as integral encounter, 75.
Sociology, should be a normative science, 67.
Subjectivism, 52.

TECHNOLOGY, 54 f.; 57, 75.
Theology, and the philosophy of Encounter, 77 ff.
Thing-Knowledge, primacy of, 4 ff.; attempt to reduce knowledge of man to, 15. See also *Knowledge.*

IMPRIMATUR

Nihil Obstat
     Francis A. Vermeulen O.S.A., S.T.D.
         Censor Deputatus

Imprimi Potest
     Hubert J. Kobessen O.S.A., S.T.D.
         Vicarius Provincialis

Imprimatur
     Mathew A.P.J. Oomens
         Vicarius Generalis Diocesis Buscoducensis